...cks underneath a hoop skirt. Book one

Excerpt from
# Bricks underneath a Hoop Skirt

*My horse, Whiskey, cautiously stepped into the water. It came almost to his belly. I held my feet out, still in the stirrups, and lifted the reins. Slowly, Whiskey picked his way towards the opposite bank.*

*The creek had risen drastically in the four days I'd been in hunting camp. Snow had fallen steadily that November, melting off during the peak of each day and pooling deepest at the crossing near the trailhead, where the truck and stock trailer had been parked. Briefly I wondered if I was going to end up trapped in a canvas tent for the winter, alone with a guide and a hunter. Before too much longer, we might be unable to cross.*

*The water cascaded in wide, white waves around mossy rocks and fallen tree trunks. It pooled briefly at Whiskey's fuzzy legs before surging around a bend between the pines. Sheets of ice spread from banks where yellowed foliage was so thick, the early morning sun didn't reach it. Blue puffs of steam came out of Whiskey's nostrils as he lifted and set one hoof at a time against the slick spots beneath him.*

*"Loooooord, it's cold," I muttered to myself, holding the neck of my wool coat closed with one hand. I should have been alone in camp, reading a book in-between hauling and heating water, splitting and carrying firewood, straightening and sweeping out the tents, and fixing a hot soup for lunch. But the hunter had left his shaving kit behind, and someone had to fetch it.*

*I watched the muscles rippling in Whiskey's shoulders. Stocky, gentle, and dependable, he had been a great mount for me during the few weeks I'd worked as cook for a Montana outfitter. Trusting the little horse completely, I rocked back and forth to his movements as the dirt trail loomed closer.*

*Suddenly, Whiskey slipped.*

*His head completely disappeared as his knees struck the creek bottom. A huge wave of water cascaded over the tips of his ears, hitting my torso with the force of a dozen ice buckets. Water gushed down my neck, back, stomach and legs and pooled in my rubber, felt-lined boots. Gasping, I clawed for the saddle horn. "Sheeeeeiii....." echoed through the forest as an automatic response to the shock.*

*Whiskey lurched, scrambling to regain his footing, and the action flung me backwards like a cowboy on a bronc. My hat flipped off and I stretched over his rump, groping wildly with one hand to snatch for it. By the time I'd wrapped my fingers around the brim he'd made it to the trail opening, gotten his footing in the mud and sand and started churning up the hill.*

*A slender Aspen tree had fallen at the highest point — we ducked underneath it when packing into camp — but now, forgotten in the emergency, it made direct contact with my head as I straightened in the saddle. For a second it felt like the scalp had been completely ripped off. Flung backwards yet again I yelped, clapped one hand to my head, and immediately checked the glove for blood.*

*Single-mindedly, Whiskey went straight for the rig thata was parked thirty yards away, sliding to a halt at the trailer. I slumped forward, moaning and massaging my noggin. He briefly glanced backward before shaking himself as vigorously as a dog. My hat hit the ground and I slowly and painfully climbed down from the saddle to save it before it got stepped on.*

*It would not be the last time Mother Nature got the best of me when I worked in the mountains, but it was certainly one of the most memorable.*

What people are saying about popular columnist and freelancer Carolyn White's new memoire,

## Bricks underneath a Hoop Skirt:

*"Reading this book is like sitting around a campfire and laughing hysterically while listening to a person who has lived the stories."* – Robin Davis, Editor, RDH EDITING

*"Carolyn has a knack for finding unusual stories and she loves to connect with people who march to their own drummers. You might find inspiration in this book for your own 'out of the box' experience or hobby. At the least, you'll enjoy spending time with the subjects of these fine stories."* — Mark Newhall, Editor & Publisher, FARM SHOW magazine

*"Don't let the self-deprecation in Carolyn White's humor fool you; she writes about the West with knowing detail that can come only from riding deep and living rough in its forested depths. Along the way, the people she encounters are as entertaining as the horses, and both species get up to no end of antics. Here you have beauty, hardship, and laughs, way out in the wilderness."* — Steve Bunk, Editor, IDAHO Magazine

*"Carolyn White's passion for her subject matter shines through her writing. Her love of history, her curiosity, and meticulous research of her subject matter make her writings worthy of a lengthy sit down in your favorite reading chair on a cold winter's night, preferably with a warm beverage."* Mike Rosso, owner and editor, COLORADO CENTRAL magazine

*"My husband, Tom, and I were waiting at the ranch's trailhead when we heard the harness jingling. There came Carolyn down the wagon trail, all by herself, driving a huge team of horses. Taking that ride back to the lodge with her, sitting up high and watching the scenery unfold, was just amazing. So was the three-day camping trip we made to the Salmon River on horseback. It was the vacation of a lifetime."* Jody Bigger Brookover, ranch guest and friend.

*"College friend Carolyn, known as "CC", invited this city girl to spend time with her at a backcountry lodge. Little did I know I'd be turned into "Pioneer Woman." She taught me how to milk a cow, saddle and ride a mule, help hitch a horse-drawn wagon, cut wood for different stoves, and cook meals on a gorgeous woodstove. She definitely gave this city girl a good education."* Katie "KT" Kirchner Grgetic, ranch guest and friend.

# Bricks underneath a Hoop Skirt

## Book One

CAROLYN WHITE

Cover photo by Nancy Coleman
Back cover photo by Carolyn White
Author contact: darby@unleashedpublishingco.com
Follow us on Face Book under **Carolyn White Book and Magazine Stories**

LifeRich Publishing is a registered trademark of The Reader's Digest Association, Inc.

LifeRich Publishing books may be ordered through booksellers or by contacting:

LifeRich Publishing
1663 Liberty Drive
Bloomington, IN 47403
www.liferichpublishing.com
1 (888) 238-8637

ISBN: 978-1-4897-1637-8 (sc)
ISBN: 978-1-4897-1638-5 (hc)
ISBN: 978-1-4897-1636-1 (e)

Library of Congress Control Number: 2018939269

Print information available on the last page.

LifeRich Publishing rev. date: 04/05/2018

*For John Waller,*
Who came back into my life 17 years after we parted
in McCall, Idaho, and upon hearing I wanted to finish
writing a book about the backcountry, simply said,
"You can do it. I believe in you…I always have."

*In memory of the late Marge Bertram*
Who reminded me the greatest of friendships
are ageless, accepting, loving, and kind.

# ACKNOWLEDGEMENTS

The nostalgia of the ranch has been replaced with electricity, telephone, mail service, and a paved road; for that reason, the name and location haven't been revealed. To the crew, thanks for watching my back, making me laugh, and helping heave heavy packs onto tall horses and mules. Mark, I never meet a Minnesotan without recalling how you wore T-shirts in below-freezing temperatures while shaming us with, "You call this cold?" Travis, when I hear that name I think of what everyone called you: "Travvie-Ravvis." And Pat, I hope you're still doing that woodwork.

To the outdoorsy, home-town friends whom I adored (and frequently went riding, camping, caving, or back-packing with) — Leigh, Missy, Stacy, Alison, Martha, Debbie, Karen, Mindy, Helen, Heidi, Lora, Janie, Trish, Karen, Jody, Bob S., Chip, Steve "Q", Tisha, John G., Kevin, Debra, Kim, Peter, Jay, and all the Mullens (if I left out anyone, I'll make note of it in book two) — thanks for making those growing-up years so memorable. For the rest of my life, hardwood trees in the fall, campfires, outrageous comments and laughter, star-filled nights, and full moons will remain the most wonderful things in the world.

To my sister Nancy, thank you for carefully and diligently reading through and critiquing my initial stories — even when you were so tired from working all day (and taking care of Mom) you could barely talk. I have never met anyone so consistently loving, encouraging, and thoughtful.

To my brother, Lewis, you were my hero during childhood for bandaging bloody knees, giving piggyback rides, and sneaking me bubble gum (I had a retainer, so chewy things were forbidden). You remain my hero today with your wisdom, honesty, and unwavering sense of honor.

To my boss at Cedaredge Pharmacy, John B., thanks for allowing me to freely answer cell phone calls from editors or stopping whatever I was (supposed to be) doing to write down antidotes for this book. I also appreciate the endless agricultural leads you suggested for magazine material.

Thanks to Annette, who filled in as "pleasure" proof-reader, Robin, who continued editing even during vacation, Markee, who always made herself available when I needed a computer whiz, and Mari-Emilie, who printed endless copies at the library.

Thank you, Emily, Ryan, Melissa, Peggy, and Craig for taking my dog every weekend so she wouldn't go crazy with boredom while I stared at the computer. Thank you, Cassandra, for always instinctively knowing when it was time for Girl Night, dinner, and catch-up. (FYI we're on for Mexico...)

Thank you, Leigh, for proofing almost every single chapter here in addition to the magazine assignments I got writer's block on. You not only gave your time freely, but you tossed out wonderful suggestions — and strong warnings about the over-use of commas — along the way. I *will* buy us a European cruise someday...but let's see how this book does first, okay?

To Vern and Connie, who took me on the Grand Canyon mule ride in May 2017, thanks for helping to rekindle the love of riding, camping, and in this case, beating people at cards. Soundly.

To favorite magazine editors, Steve Bunk at *IDAHO Magazine*, Mark Newhall at *Farm Show*, Mike Rosso at *Colorado Central*, and the original editor of the Western Slope edition of *The Fence Post*, Brian Soule: I will always appreciate that you guys bought every single story, column, or interview I sent and barely changed a word.

Finally, in memory of English and Creative Writing teachers Doris Curtis and Clark Murphy at Marietta Senior High School in Marietta, Ohio, I'd like to say that little is more important to a teenager than someone who "sees" and empowers them while expecting the best.

Carolyn White
February 2018

# CONTENTS

# PROLOGUE
## CENTRAL IDAHO
## MID-1990'S

It gets brutally cold during high mountain winters, sometimes dropping to 30 below zero with well over 160 inches of snowfall — enough to bury entire houses. Solid sheets of ice form over windows and sliding glass doors. Winds roar all night long. The sun disappears under thick, low-hanging clouds. Roads stay slick for months.

It's not a life for sissies.

Wood stove heat is the only thing that cuts through those bone-chilling conditions. An advantage such a stove is you can hang damp clothing around it to dry, leave a pot of water on it to humidify the air, and in a pinch (like when the power lines collapse under weight of snow), cook on it. The downside is one must cut, stack, split, and carry *a lot* of firewood to last an entire season. It's dirty, tedious, back-breaking, and if you aren't careful, dangerous work. But before moving to the tiny logging town of McCall, Idaho I'd already grown accustomed to it.

Firewoodin' was a constant weekend activity during spring, summer and fall in rugged places like that. (Combined, those three seasons lasted maybe four months, tops.) In convoys, my friends and I drove to wherever there was a decent supply of deadfall and we filled every pickup truck and trailer to the point they nearly scraped the ground. By the end of the day we were completely worn out and covered with pitch, dirt, sawdust and (occasionally) spiders and ticks. But there was nothing quite as satisfying as stacking a huge pile of logs in one's yard, covering it with a tarp, and heading towards the house with an armload, knowing you'd be warm.

Deadfall was often pulled from clearings that were very hard to reach. Most were scouted out during hunting or mushroom seasons, when folks were either on foot or horseback. Some of those old, overgrown roads our trucks bounced over were so steep, the tires lost traction and the rear end fish-tailed. Going downhill, to keep from losing control one shifted to low-low gear and tapped the brakes. If the mud holes or snow drifts got deep, you stepped out and locked each wheel hub into four-wheel-drive. And of course, in those sections where the mountains went straight up on one side and straight down on the other, it was best to *not* look down.

Once the chainsaws had been fired up by the men — the whine of the blades rising and falling as they cut — we women efficiently hustled back and forth to heave rounds, haul them to the rigs, and dump them noisily into the scarred metal beds. The heavier rounds, we rolled or pushed with our boots.

If a sawn tree was high on a hill, the younger kids rolled wood towards us. "HEADS UP!" they were trained to yell as a warning. Logs often came bouncing and careening crazily downward, gathering so much speed they blasted right past us. Once, however, as I was turning, an especially large one made direct contact with my right shin. It hurt so bad I thought it was broken. Gasping and clutching that leg, I hopped about yipping "Owie owie owie owieeeeeeeeeeeee!" until one of the men, Will, glanced up from the tailgate of a nearby truck where he'd been sharpening his saw blades.

"You okay?" he asked casually, without stopping. I recall he had a wad of tobacco in one cheek and was wearing his baseball cap backwards.

"Noooooooo...owie owie owie oooooooooooohhhhh, owie owie owie"...I moaned, sinking onto a stump and vigorously rubbing the shin. Glancing uphill, I caught the eyes of the pre-teen who had launched the round without shouting out. She raised her shoulders to both ears, clearly indicating, 'Duh. What a moron.'

'I'm gonna kill you,' I thought peevishly, but instead of communicating that I gazed back at her and lightly smacked my forehead with the heel of one hand.

Observing the exchange, Will said matter-of-factly, "You gotta be tough to live in the mountains." He reached for an oil can.

Instantly, my mind flashed to the remote guest ranch I'd lived on before moving back to civilization the previous year. I saw Jim and Shorty, the Belgian draft horse team, dragging thick, massive tree trunks from the forest to the wood shed with their hoof tips digging into the dirt, their hindquarters straining, and their tug chains rattling sharply. I felt the shoulder-jarring connection of an axe head striking against a splitting maul. I felt the heat coming from the opened door of a barrel stove as wood was stuffed inside, and the cool from an opened kitchen window as jugs of warm, fresh milk were stuffed into snow banks to cool.

I remembered breaking ice in the creek and lugging endless buckets of water through waist-high snow after pipes froze. Of being caught in storms while on horseback, riding with the collar of an outback coat turned up against piercing sleet. Unsaddling horses and mules with fingers which were so frozen I couldn't feel them. Wearing a cap, socks, and thermal underwear to bed on sub-zero nights in a century-old cabin.

How deeply I'd loved living like a modern-day pioneer; it was the experience of a lifetime. Fortunately, in McCall it sometimes felt like I was still back there.

I must have seemed a thousand miles away as I sat idly massaging my leg because Will stopped and leaned forward. "Sure you're okay?" he asked.

"Yes. I'm fine." There was a skiff of snow nearby, and easing my pant leg up, I scooped a handful and carefully placed it on the skin. An enormous bruise had already started forming in faint purples, yellows and greens. Waiting for the throbbing to ebb, I watched the dozen or so men, women and children — each wearing heavy boots, flannel shirts, hats, jackets, and work gloves — swarming the hillside. *Mmmmrrrrrrrrrruuuuuuummmm, mmmmmrrrrrrrrruuuuuum, mmrrrrUUUUUUUMMMMMMM* sounds and assorted shouts echoed in the air, and acrid blue smoke lingered overhead. With dull, metallic *thunks,* rounds were being dumped into truck beds. On their knees, stackers twisted and turned at the waist to pull and push those logs towards the tight rows they were organizing. Everyone was covered with mud, moss, twigs and sap.

Reaching for one of several community water jugs, I took a drink and wiped my mouth with the back of one hand, discreetly spitting sawdust. I lowered my pant leg, stood slowly and rocked back and forth, testing the injury. "Gonna make it?" Will persisted, raising one eyebrow.

"I think so." The shin hurt so bad I figured the bone was at least dented (it still hurts off and on) but it supported my weight okay.

Will gestured towards the others with his funnel. "Sit if you need to. There's plenty of people helping. We'll get it done."

I stared over his head for a moment, watching the Tamarack and Ponderosa pines swaying in a brisk, rising wind. "Thanks, but I'll be fine," I assured him.

"Okay." He shrugged and resumed focus on the chainsaw. Powering through the pain, I gimped off to join the others.

# CHAPTER 1

# WHISKEY AND WATER

My horse, Whiskey, cautiously stepped into the water. It came almost to his belly. I held my feet out, still in the stirrups, and lowered the reins. Slowly, Whiskey picked his way towards the opposite bank.

Snow had fallen steadily that November, melting off during the peak of each day and pooling deepest at the crossing near the trailhead, where the truck and stock trailer had been parked. The creek had risen drastically in the four days I'd been in hunting camp. Briefly I wondered if I was going to end up trapped in a canvas tent for the winter, alone with a guide and a hunter. Before too much longer, we might be unable to cross.

The water cascaded in wide, white waves around rocks and fallen tree trunks. It pooled briefly at Whiskey's fuzzy legs before roaring around a bend between the pines. Sheets of ice spread from the banks where yellowed foliage was so thick, the early morning sun didn't reach it. Blue puffs of steam came out of Whiskey's nostrils as he lifted and set one hoof at a time against the slick spots beneath him.

"*Loooooord*, it's cold," I muttered to myself. I should have been alone in camp, reading a book in-between hauling and heating water, doing dishes, splitting and carrying firewood, straightening and sweeping out the tents, and fixing a hot soup for lunch. But the hunter had left his shaving kit behind, and someone had to fetch it.

I watched the muscles rippling in Whiskey's shoulders. Stocky, sure-footed, and gentle, he had been a great mount for me during the few weeks I'd been working as cook for a Montana outfitter. Trusting the little horse completely, I swayed back and forth to his movements as the dirt trail loomed closer.

Suddenly, Whiskey slipped.

His head completely disappeared as his knees struck the creek bottom. A huge wave of water cascaded over the tips of his ears, hitting my torso with the force of a dozen ice buckets. Instantly, water gushed down my neck, back, stomach and legs and pooled in my rubber, felt-lined boots. Gasping, I clawed for the saddle horn with one hand while swiping at my face with the other. "Sheeeee....." echoed through the forest as an automatic response to the shock.

Whiskey lurched up and down, scrambling to regain his footing, and the action flung me backwards like a cowboy on a bronc. My hat flipped off and I stretched over his rump, groping wildly with one hand to snatch it before it was swept away. By the time I'd wrapped my fingers around the brim he'd made it to the trail opening, gotten his footing in the mud and sand and started churning up the hill.

A slender Aspen tree had fallen at the highest point — we'd all ducked underneath it when packing into camp — but now, forgotten in the emergency, as I straightened in the saddle it made direct contact with my forehead. For a moment it felt like the scalp had been completely ripped off. Flung backwards yet again I yelped, clapped one hand to my head, and checked the glove for blood.

Single-mindedly, Whiskey went straight for the rig that was parked thirty yards away, sliding to a halt at the trailer. I slumped forward and leaned over the saddle horn, moaning and massaging my noggin. He briefly glanced backward before shaking himself as vigorously as a dog. My hat hit the ground and I slowly and painfully climbed down from the saddle to save it before it got stepped on.

It was not the last time Mother Nature got the best of me when I worked in the mountains, but it was certainly one of the most memorable.

During any given hour in the mountains it can switch from sun to rain to snow and back to sun again. One had to be prepared, keeping raingear tied behind the cantle of the saddle, a wool coat tied in front of the horn and a bandana, a wool cap and dry socks tucked into saddlebags. I never went without thermal underwear (or a one-piece red union suit) during winter and fall, and always slipped bread bags over my feet for extra insulation on the coldest of days. If temps barely hovered above zero, I even spread an extra horse blanket across my lap before heading out to camp. Layers were the trick, and sometimes they made all the difference in the world — especially when you spent eight to ten days at a time in a tent.

An outfitter's campsites were primitive at best. It was a tedious job to set one up, even when the weather was clear. Usually it was either raining, snowing, or sleeting, and there were few experiences more miserable than slogging through the mud while chopping down seven lodgepole pines, stripping them of branches and needles, wiring them together in two A-frames, setting the center pole, heaving a sodden, smelly, heavy canvas tent into the air, bracing it, pulling out the five-foot sidewalls, and tying them off to support beams.

Getting a fire started under such conditions also tested the endurance. (Eventually I started carrying extra newspaper, matches, and kindling in a zip lock bag so they'd be dry. Otherwise you'd get enough smoke to send signals.) Dampness soaks right through your clothing when you're working outside, no matter what you have on, and once you're cold it takes long, long time to get warm again.

It was an entirely different sensation along the Salmon River, which was hot hot *hot*. During summer, temperatures hit triple digits. The sun burned the backs of your neck and hands. And rattlesnakes emerged from their cool, rocky hiding places to warm up, surprising me several times. (Once you've hear that ominous rattle, you never forget it.)

I remember taking guests on three-day, two-night rides from the mountain peaks to the river, feeling it growing warmer and warmer the lower we went. By their second afternoon in the saddle, folks were so dirty they *clamored* for showers. We got what was available.

While exploring the creek bank, I'd found a quiet eddy that was heavily surrounded and shaded by willows. This was a huge score because it offered privacy. The water came up to the waist and there was a wide, dry rock ledge for setting soap, towels, clean clothes and whatever else a body needed. Tell you what, though, that outdoor tub was *cooooold*. It didn't matter how much trail dirt, horse hair, bridle slime, or mud a person was wearing, one couldn't stay in the water any longer than what was absolutely necessary. Those of us on the crew could be in and out in a minute or less apiece. But we never warned the dudes. It was too much fun to hear a splash followed by "Eeeeeeeeeeeeeeaaaaaaaaaaooooooooowwww!"

The water of the Salmon River was exceptionally cold, too. I walked across it once...no, make that twice...during a Bighorn sheep hunt in August. I'd gone along to cook, having no idea how challenging it would be. While glassing the area with binoculars, the hunter and his guide had spotted a herd of ewes on the opposite bank and figured there'd be a ram close-by. Barefoot, with our jeans rolled up and our boots tied to already-heavy backpacks, we crossed the water one at a time. Even though the clear green water was low that year due to drought — and I'd picked a stout branch to use as a brace — the flow of it against my calves was extraordinarily powerful. One misstep could have led to a fall, and once a person went down...well, I tried not to think about that. Instead, I focused on placing each cold, numb bare foot down as carefully as a tightrope walker with no net, glancing upward only to gauge my progress towards the beach. Once that beach was reached, the sense of euphoria was overwhelming until I realized that eventually, we'd have to go back the way we'd come.

Silently, I cursed the guys and their binoculars.

We camped outside that night, not bothering to set up nylon tents because it was so warm out. But the sun set early behind the steep ranges that towered around us. Temperatures dropped 30 degrees... maybe more. Beyond the campfire light, pitch-darkness enveloped us because smoke from local forest fires obscured the moon and stars. I'd been sweating for days, hiking unshaded trails that were carved into harsh, rocky hillsides. That night, I got so cold I pulled the hood of my goose down mummy bag around my head and tightened the cords. The next morning, we woke to a covering of frost and soot everything. Getting up to re-kindle the fire, break ice in the kettle and put the coffee on to boil was nothing less than pure, teeth-chattering torture.

During that arduous experience we climbed over 3,000 feet and covered nearly thirty miles round-trip in relentless sun while scoping for brown sheep against a brown background, breathing brown smoke, eating powdered dinners (that never quite filled the stomach), drinking warm water from canteens, and wearing dirty clothing every day. (I did manage to rinse mine out while at the river.) We saw only one ram, on the sixth. The hunter raised and lowered his rifle several times before deciding against shooting. The curl wasn't long or thick enough for him.

Initially, I couldn't believe it. *What*? We'd hiked *how* far? In *that* kind of heat? Then I felt relief. It would have been awful to trudge back to the nearest airstrip, where a pilot had arranged to pick us up, carrying boned-out meat.

Anyhow, the good part of the experience was when I got back to the ranch, the crew was impressed when they heard all we went through. They started treating me differently, like I was one of the guys. And bonus, I lost five pounds from so much hiking.

Packing meat for hunters and dealing with harsh weather was part of the job — but being sent out in a freeze for a shaving kit really rubbed me the wrong way. After retrieving my hat from under Whiskey's belly, I collapsed against the trailer's nearest fender, removed the soaked gloves and carefully pressed icy fingers against the egg that was forming on my forehead. It brought no relief. Groaning, I leaned over and unlaced each boot, removed them, inverted everything, and shook the water out. The liners were completely soaked; I'd have to leave them as they were.

Trying to decide what to do next, I stared at Whiskey. He took a deep breath, blew it out, and shifted, waiting patiently for me to load him into the trailer and haul him someplace warm. At least that's what I figured he was thinking. I considered starting the truck and turning on the heater but knew that would be futile. No way would blower heat dry anything. (Besides, we'd need all the remaining gas to drive out of the mountains.) Bitter cold was seeping through my bones, slowing my movements and muddling my mind. What I needed was to remove all that wet clothing and raise my body temperature as quickly as possible.

Stiffly I rose, unlocked the truck, shoved the bench seat forward, and groped for the shaving kit. My clothes were completely plastered to my skin, hanging heavily, and each movement was cold, stiff and painful. Shuffling to Whiskey's rump, I set the kit down behind the saddle and jerked the leather latigos tightly around it. I tried to get my left foot in the stirrup but couldn't raise the leg high enough, so took the reins to drag Whiskey to a stump. He balked, stretching his neck out as far as it would go. His hooves dragged in the dirt like a kid being taken to the dentist.

Bouncing on my right leg a few times for momentum, I awkwardly pulled myself into the saddle, flopped forward across the horn and struggled to get upright. Whiskey took the opportunity to swerve towards the trailer one last time but I reined him around, a bit roughly. "Sorry, bud," I said firmly, "we aren't stayin'."

He walked as if all fours had been whittled out of pogo sticks, protesting as horses do when they're being pushed. Completely running out of patience, I kicked him, hard, and urged him towards the water. Five miles lay between us, a heat source, a hay pile, and a tent... and we'd both have to make the entire trip soaking wet.

## Part 2

Stripped of nearly-frozen clothing, I balanced on the edge of the cook tent's picnic table and held both feet towards the rusted barrel stove. The vents were wide open, and it had been stuffed with every chunk of kindling I could find. Small branches had been added as needed to keep the fire as hot as possible; the stove's metal sides glowed red, mirroring the color of my skin. My teeth chattered so hard I thought the enamel would break. I couldn't feel extremities and fretted about possible frostbite. It was past 2:00 in the afternoon and temperatures had warmed to about 35 degrees, but my body felt more like sub-zero.

The sun ducked in and out of the clouds and a soft wind blew, causing the tent walls to lazily suck in and out like a giant set of lungs. The canvas crackled softly, and silhouettes of trees moved against it. Normally I would have enjoyed the quiet play of lights and shadows and the creaking of the lodge pole pines. While doing daily camp chores, I'd often stopped to admire the view. But not right then.

Whisky, rubbed down with a towel and buckled into a quilted horse blanket, stood drowsily at the hitching rail. Steam arose from his neck. Towards the end of our return trip, the ice that had formed on his mane, tail, and fetlocks had started melting and now, droplets methodically fell from the coarse hairs. It had taken every ounce of energy and determination I had left to remove his gear and make sure he'd been taken care of. First rule (my own) was to always put the livestock first. But *oh!* that whole ride had been miserable — by far the most miserable one I've ever experienced.

The thawing trail had turned to ankle-deep mud in some areas, and the gelding was forced to go slow to keep from sliding. At the worst spots, he'd picked the way with muzzle down, carefully choosing the least-mucky routes. Part of me had hoped we'd make record time getting back to camp (since horses tend to go faster when heading home). Instead it was like taking the slow boat to China.

Earlier in the week I'd done a small load of laundry in a dish pan, squeezed things out and draped them over the tent's support poles. That night, I forgot to bring the clothing inside and everything froze. After bending the long johns and flannel shirt into absurd, people-like poses, I took pictures and laughed out loud at my own silliness. (Hey, when you're alone all day, you learn to entertain yourself.) Now, I felt just like one of those garments: frozen and forgotten, but in this case, definitely un-funny.

No one had been at camp when I returned. Usually the guide and hunter petered out between ten and eleven each morning and returned to eat and nap before leaving again. However, there was no welcoming smoke from the chimney. Nobody hustled out to fuss over me. No food had been prepared. No one took Whiskey, tying him and lugging his saddle and bridle into the blue canvas tack shack. No one lay the wet saddle pad, inverted, in a sunny spot to dry. No one bent over to dig mud out of his hooves, and no one brought him hay.

The only, single day (to that point) there'd been a serious need for help I was completely on my own. And to add insult to injury, for Pete's Sake, *it was my flippin' birthday*! I should have been spending it warm as toast in a tent with the flaps tied tightly, propped up on the cot while reading a good book and sipping a cup of coffee, thoroughly enjoying my quiet time. But noooooooooooooooooooo, I'd had to clean the tent after 6:00 am breakfast, bundle up, saddle a horse, and ride down the mountain on a sub-zero day to fetch some dude his stupid shaving kit.

He'd have been better off starting a beard like a real man.

Wincing, I stepped onto the plastic floor (standing on discarded clothes), leaned over, and held both arms about an inch from the stove in an attempt to absorb more heat. If I could have hugged it without searing the torso, I would have. For an hour I rotated like a chicken on a spit, alternating feet, legs, back, arms, and belly while waiting for feeling to return*. I'd also tried to dry my hair, which dripped like Whiskey's fetlocks. Muttering, I reached down for more firewood, shoved it into the blazing firebox, slammed the door shut, and separated the dank, heavy hair mass into sections, attempting to speed the process.

Whiskey whinnied, high and shrill, and it startled me. Muffled hoofbeats and the sounds of laughing male voices could be heard in the distance. Hastily, I dove into the fresh clothes that had been laid out on the table, fumbling at buttons, zippers and laces with fingers that were still stiff.

Untying the flaps to the cook tent, I peered out in time to see Wesley, the hunter, and Don, his guide, dismounting at the hitching rail. Right away I noticed their wool jackets were bloody. Forgetting aggravation, I hurried outside with the laces of my tennis shoes trailing. "Did you get an elk?" I asked excitedly.

"No, we did better than that," Wesley grinned. Wearing a green-checkered flannel shirt and wool cap, with dirty blond hair sticking out of the sides and hazel eyes dancing, he looked more like a ten-year-old kid than a thirty-something construction worker. "I shot a bear."

"*What*?" Although he'd gotten a tag, it was late in the year. Most bears had started to hibernate by then, so we didn't expect he would see anything.

"Yup. It was a big one, too," he added with enthusiasm.

Don, a salt-and-pepper haired guy who also worked as a taxidermist, added, "It's a Black bear, but it's going to take a small grizzly frame to mount the hide."

"No kidding! Where is it? What color was it?" A blond-colored Black bear had been brought in earlier that season, and it had been gorgeous. I craned my neck to see if either of the horses had anything tossed over them.

The bear, they explained in-between unhooking their rifle scabbards and unsaddling, was jet-black with a small circle of white on its chest. They'd happened across it in the forest. After we settled in the cook tent, I brewed coffee and made sandwiches while the men took turns telling the complete story.

While tracking an elk through a grove of spruce trees they heard a strange, gasping noise. "It was like a huffing sound," Wesley described, gesturing to his broad chest and patting it briskly, "huhhuhhuhhuhhuhhuhhuhhuh — real rapid-like."

"Yeah, like this..." Don added his own version. "Whuhwhoowhuwhoowhuh. We followed the noise to check it out."

What they found was a deeply trampled spot in a meadow and two blood trails. One went off into the forest and the other led to a lone Ponderosa standing at the edge of a draw. The pine was dead, and most of the needles had fallen off, so when they looked up they easily spotted the bear.

"It was clear it had gotten into a scuffle with my bull," Wesley said. "Blood was flowing out of a huge puncture wound in its side."

I'd never heard of a bull elk fighting a bear but knew antlers could be deadly. "What happened next?" I asked breathlessly.

Don shrugged. "It was suffering, so Wes put it out of its misery. It dropped to the ground at our feet" ...he elbowed Wesley, who looked sheepish for a second... "and rolled straight down into the draw."

It had taken both men, a horse, and a couple of hours to drag the body back to level ground. Don, an Idaho native, luckily had a rope and he'd tied it around his waist, wrapped the excess around the tree trunk, and eased backwards down the hillside. With the bear wedged between two boulders, Don awkwardly braced against a juniper bush and gutted it. He then untied the lasso from his own waist, secured it around the carcass, and shoved while Wesley pulled. Twice, Don lost his footing and almost slid to the bottom of the draw. The going was so tough, Wesley finally fetched one of the horses, untied the tree end of the lasso and dallied it around the saddle horn. (He had to blindfold the nervous animal first, since the bear smell made it skittish). Don precariously supported the carcass, kicking footholds in exposed roots and moist dirt for leverage, until it was safe to start shoving again.

"We'll go back tomorrow morning with a mule to pack the bear out," Don concluded, reaching towards the plate I'd set before them.

"Yeah, and maybe we'll find that wounded elk, too," Wesley added teasingly.

"Don't push it," Don said, but he was smiling.

Wesley drained his cup of coffee, reached for a second sandwich, and swung his legs over the bench seat. Standing, he briefly stretched before hastily dropping both arms. "Yuk, I can smell myself. Sweaty Man and Dead Bear..."

"Maybe we should bottle that," Don observed with his mouth full.

Wes jabbed at him with one foot before continuing, "Carolyn, can I use that hot water on the stove? I need a bath, bad."

"Sure." I rose, lifted the metal bucket up with a few hot pads and carefully poured water into the wash tub.

"Save some for me," Don said as Wesley jammed the sandwich between his teeth, lifted the tub and turned to leave.

"Get your own, I'm using *all* of this!" Wesley sassed, his voice muffled through the bread. But he wasn't gone for two minutes before sticking his face through the flaps again. "Hey, did you get my shaving kit?"

"*Did I?*" I placed both hands on my hips. "Maybe you'd better hear what *I* went through today while trying to fetch it!"

The guide and the hunter listened attentively, often cringing, as I described Whiskey's dive into the water, the direct hit of the wave, the sensation of ice forming on my ears, neck, face, and body, and the unbearably sloppy, slow ride back to camp.

"Man, I'm glad you're all right," Don said sincerely after I'd finished. "People can drown even in shallow water. *Especially* this time of year. It's so cold it takes your breath away and you can't make it to shore."

"No kidding," I responded sarcastically, "try riding inside an ice block." I gestured to the clothing that hung from nails by the stove. "*That* will take your breath away, too! I was so frozen when I got back here I started the fire, stripped, and stood like this..." I demonstrated, bending at the waist and pretending to hug the barrel, "trying to defrost!"

The men glanced at each other. Wesley ran a palm over the scruff on his chin and idly scratched it. Don stuffed the remaining corner of a sandwich into his mouth and washed it down with coffee. I waited for one of them to exclaim, "Great job!" and tell me what a trooper I'd been — how brave and strong and amazing. How tough. At least they could thank me for risking my life to fetch shaving cream, a razor, a pair of toenail clippers, a toothbrush, and toothpaste. But for the longest time, both men were silent.

Instead, Wesley leaned forward and murmured directly into Don's ear, "Hey, buddy, I didn't really need to get a bear. It's going to cost a fortune to mount. Maybe we should have come back to camp sooner."

*Don't try this at home. I learned later that the best way to deal with frostbite is to gently and gradually thaw the extremities in warm water. Luckily, I didn't have it. Probably wouldn't be typing this with all ten fingers if that had been the case.

*"Wet camp clothes were left to drip-dry outside a tent."*

# CHAPTER 2

---

# GRADUATION DAY

(Versions of this story appeared in both my *Fence Post* column, "Living the Good Life," and in the June 2016 issue of *IDAHO Magazine*.)

Our trainer in Guide School had warned us that saddle horses, tied together on a trail, are among the stupidest animals on earth. "Hitch a seasoned pack mule between 'em and they're usually fine," he pointed out after stuffing tobacco into his lip, "but left on their own, they turn plum' idiot."

Instead of quietly and steadily following nose-to-tail like mules did, a horse was bound to stop and gawk at something, or lean down to scratch a leg, or idly go around the opposite side of a tree of the horse in front of it. Its head would bang against the bark, its eyes would go wild and then *SNAP,* the piggin' string — a length of hay-baling twine that attached it to the animal ahead — would break as it pulled back in a panic. The newly-freed horse was then free to wander through the dense forest, dragging along whatever others were tied behind it, until *they* ended up going around the opposite sides of trees, banging the bark, planting their hooves, and breaking their piggin' strings, too.

For the final test before getting a license to guide, pack, and cook, each student had to lead a string of three saddle horses from base camp to a high mountain fishing spot. I wasn't worried a bit. Tightening my mare, Tee's*, cinch by pulling it straight up (instead of out like the boys did, which made their animals rock back and forth) I thought, 'Piece of cake.' After all, I'd grown up with horses, exploring endless hardwood forest trails, jogging along quiet country roads, or racing my friends across open meadows. That gave me the edge over the other students, most of whom had had little to no experience (outside of watching Westerns) before showing up in Idaho.

The guide school course, which took place at a drive-to campsite about 18 miles off Lolo Pass, had been easy from the start. In addition to mule packing, we learned how to read topographical maps, set up tents, dig latrines, and start camp fires in pouring rain. (I'd already done that stuff with my friends growing up.) We learned that the most dangerous animal in the forest was a bull moose in rut, and the quickest way to bring in an elk was to bugle overtop him, before he'd finished his own shrill call. We learned to open and close coolers quickly, taking whatever meat was on top; that elk was better than venison because "deer eat everything, and it tastes like it, but elk are grass-grazers"; and that bear meat, if not handled and cooked properly, was really, *reeeeaaaally* awful.

I learned a lot about food preparation during training, mostly by the sink or swim method. As the only female, it was expected that I stick close to the mess tent. (The guy students hadn't exactly welcomed me; instead, they treated me more like an intruder. During the First Aid class we were sent to in Lewiston, one jerk even copped a squeeze of my rear.) But the joke was on them. I couldn't cook. They got runny spaghetti for supper one evening and bloody chicken another. Being 100 miles from the closest town, there were no grocery stores or pizza places to run to for back-up, so sometimes it was pork and beans.

When the propane tanks ran out I had no choice but cook outside over an open pit. Breakfast pancakes were particularly troublesome. For one thing, it's impossible to balance a griddle adequately over rocks, no matter how flat they are, so the batter spreads unevenly. The griddle must be rotated constantly to keep an even heat, which means your face is in the fire. If it isn't hot enough, you end up with something white and inedible or if it's too hot, something black and inedible.

Sitting on a primitive wooden bench, I'd dip a ladle into a large, green plastic bowl of batter, gingerly pour four to six dollops at a time, and wait for them to bubble (while picking floating black ash particles out of the dough). It got particularly stressful if the boys were gathered around, impatiently twirling paper plates or plastic forks and telling me what to do. (Funny, but none of them ever volunteered to take over.) Duds were tossed into the nearby huckleberry brush to be devoured by the chipmunks and black squirrels. And to give you an idea of just how many duds there actually were, it wasn't long before entire groups of the little rascals started gathering for breakfast. Some even climbed up on my back and chattered for me to hurry!

One morning I turned to find two pink hind feed clamped down on the sides of the bowl. A chipmunk was dangling above the batter, crazily scooping handfuls into his mouth. "Hey! Git outta there!" I scolded, more amused than mad. He twisted at the mid-section and froze. All I could see was his merry brown eyes; the rest of his striped face was completely covered in cream color. He obligingly launched off the bowl and scampered a few yards away, stopping to lick himself vigorously. "Leave my bowl alone," I warned him, shaking the dipper. A few dollops of pancake mix fell into the dirt and other varmints dove in to inhale them.

Briefly, I considered tossing that bowl of batter out and starting fresh but then, smiling wickedly, I kept going. The boys weren't around at that moment, and what they didn't know wouldn't hurt them.

Regardless of the cooking hassles and the attitudes of the males, guide school was a blast and I took to it like a fish tossed into water. What made it especially sweet was having Tee, my childhood horse, with me. We'd already spent a dozen years together in Ohio before travelling to Idaho. Seeing her eating hay in the corral, listening to the wind pass through the pines, watching hawks and bald eagles circle overhead, counting the stars at night, and being in the saddle nearly every single day felt so perfect, I couldn't remember living anywhere else.

Within that first week, I didn't want to leave. That's why getting an official State license was so important: you had to have one to legally work for outfitters. With a license in pocket, chances were good I'd be able to stay out West indefinitely.

On that final morning of school, after adjusting Tee's bridle and pulling her forelock through the browband, I confidently swung into the saddle. Holding the reins in my left hand and the lead horse's halter rope in the other, I checked over my right shoulder. One of the geldings was curiously staring towards the open-flap tent where the boys talked and laughed while waiting their turns. The other two horses dozed, occasionally twitching off flies. "Hup! Hup!" I called out to get their attention. Satisfied when all three heads swung in my direction, I legged

Tee and started towards the trail with the trainer following at the end of the line.

But we had barely reached the forest before those saddle geldings started giving me fits. The lead horse nearly yanked my arm out of the socket several times by dropping its head to snatch grass. The middle one kept nipping at its rear. It also repeatedly kicked at the horse behind it. Twice, it ended up with a hind leg caught over the third horse's lead rope. Simultaneously, that third horse stopped short and threw its head back to avoid getting a hoof planted in the chest. *Snap*!

It seemed like every five minutes I had yet another wreck to deal with. The trainer pulled up and silently waited, forearms crossed over the saddle horn, about a dozen times as I dismounted to fetch runaways. I tied Tee to the closest tree or huckleberry bush, picked my way over downed trees and tangled brush, hustled to get in front of the horse that was wandering, grazing, or frozen in place with a hoof jammed against the trailing lead, caught it, straightened the saddle if it had been yanked to the side, led the horse(s) back to where we'd left off, pulled fresh piggin' string out of my saddle bags, looped it around the ring behind the cantle, snaked the lead rope through the loop, lined the geldings out again in a semi-straight row, unhitched Tee, dallied her lead around my own saddle horn, swung up, took a grip on the rope attached to the halter of the first horse, called out "Hup! Hup!" so that all three fools would face forward and started back up the trail. I even put Tee into a slow jog so they'd be compelled to stay nose-to-tail but sooner or later...*snap*... off those geldings went yet again.

What started as poorly-disguised irritation grew into grumblings that got louder and louder each time I jumped down. Stumbling over and ducking under deadfall and branches, I began freely and openly cussing the stray horses, accusing them of every brainless action ever committed by a mammal. Each time I tripped, fell, or snagged one of my braids, the foul names got fouler — and of course, this only made the trio members harder and harder to catch.

The colorful phrases were still smoking in the air when the lake finally came into view and I pulled Tee up for good. Separating the geldings, I tied each to the hitching rail with enough distance in-between that if one kicked, it wouldn't strike another. Agitated, they sidestepped and swished their tails uneasily. Red-faced and sweating on that hot afternoon, I yanked off my hat, wiped a palm across my forehead and looked up at the trainer.

He said nothing at first. A ground hog chirped in the distance and stood up by its hole. Black-billed magpies flew closer in anticipation of food. My heart pounded loud in my ears. The trainer pushed his own hat back and squinted down. Then he said the words I'd been waiting to hear since first learning, during college, there was such a thing as guide school.

"Congratulations, I'm gonna pass you in this course."

In that moment, nothing I had ever learned in books mattered anymore. I was going to earn my keep doing something I was born for! Load and lead pack strings! Ride different horses and mules every day! Live in tents, cabins, and lodges! Cut trail! (And later, write about it!) I couldn't tell you where my High school or college graduation degrees are, but I still have all those licenses.

I stood by a hitching rail in the middle of the forest, exhaling deeply as the trainer's words sunk in. Joy slowly spread through my body. For a moment I thought about jumping up and down from excitement but figured it would be undignified. Nodding shortly, I responded, "Great! Thank you!"

But my smile quickly faded when the trainer added, "You now know how to curse like a true packer."

*"Pack mules wait at feeding trough."*

*Cheyenne Tee J. was a gorgeous mix of Appaloosa, Standardbred, and Thoroughbred, gray with a black mane and tail and a perfect white arrowhead mark on her forehead. I'll put more pictures on the website.

# CHAPTER 3

---

# HORSE COLORS

(A version of this appeared in the June 2011
issue of *IDAHO Magazine*.)

At first glance, Bud was just a midget of a mule — hardly an animal to be leery of, which I wasn't. When sitting on his back my feet practically touched the ground.

He showed me who was boss, however, by flipping me over his head several times. Whenever we came to oversized logs across the trail he sized them up, leaned back on his haunches and acted like he was going to jump. Instead, he froze in mid-launch, hit reverse and simultaneously dropped his head. The results were spectacular. I soared through the air with both arms out and slammed against the forest floor. Ignoring the laughter of coworkers, I picked myself up, swiped dirt and pine needles off my hands, shirt and jeans, and stomped back over to where Bud stood waiting with a look of complete innocence on his flop-eared, dark gray face.

Since none of the others wanted to ride him — and no dude could possibly handle him — by the end of summer Bud was gone. I felt kind of bad for the little bugger as he was being loaded for the auction block, but it didn't last long. There were too many other critters to throw a leg over, and not nearly enough time to figure out what made each one of them tick.

I already had a lifetime of riding experience before leaving Ohio but that didn't make much difference. An outfitter's livestock was far different from the horses and ponies I'd grown up on. For one thing, you rarely got the same mount twice in a row. (My mare, Tee, was nearly 18 when I took her to Idaho and had a touch of arthritis, so she was rotated with other horses.) For another, animals were constantly coming and going depending on gentleness, soundness, performance and whatever feed lot sales were happening in the closest town. Round pens, riding arenas and even basic warm-ups were completely unheard of: *you just got on.* Sometimes it was a real adventure to toss a saddle onto a brand-new arrival and climb aboard — especially since there were many miles to travel and you didn't know what to expect.

The first outfitter who hired me, fresh out of guide school, merely needed someone to babysit ten horses and mules for a while. He drove me down a steep, curvy stretch of mountain road and left me at a drop camp in the middle of nowhere. (For the record, "drop camp" is the perfect name. It refers to a place that is surrounded by forest and has no phone, no electric lights, no housing beyond tents, and no tap water. Not even a dog. He said he'd be back in "about five days" with the rest of the supplies, the crew and several archery hunters. It was more like two weeks.) I drank out of a stream. Since no stove had been set up yet, I ate peanut butter sandwiches. To fill time I split firewood, raked pine needles, picked burrs out of manes and tails, and read a few stained paperbacks that had been stuffed into camp boxes.

The ten horses and mules were enclosed by a battery-powered electric fence and fed from a plastic-covered hay pile. (Twice a day I led them, two at a time, to the creek to be watered.) The outfitter never turned them loose to graze, he said, because he didn't want any to founder. Naturally, because the grass is always greener on the other side, those five mules and five horses quickly figured out ways to escape. They did it in the middle of the night, too, heading off in different directions and becoming nearly invisible within the thick groves of pine trees and Aspens.

With halters flung over both shoulders, at daybreak I sought them out and maneuvered all ten back to camp. While they waited, tied to trees, I gingerly walked the fence line trying to locate what had grounded the wire. (Turned out the car battery that powered the electricity was low on fluid...but I didn't find *that* out until the third time the herd escaped.) By then I'd had a brainstorm: catch the lead mare first and ride her home with the others following. Her name was June and she was a mahogany bay with white hind socks, a lopsided blaze and a droopy lower lip. Initially, she seemed fine with that plan. She stood calmly while I swung the rope over her neck, snugged it to the halter ring and leapt up on her back, landing on my stomach. At that exact moment June spun with the lightening precision of a Quarter horse, making two full circles without moving her hind legs. Once again, I launched, this time landing in the brush.

Heck with what I'd been told to do. I left the horses free to graze during daytime, taking a book along and keeping an eye on them.

Another temporary place, this one along the Salmon River, had the most beautiful black gelding you've ever seen. "Mind if I take that one?" I spontaneously asked the outfitter as we stood by the corral.

"Sure, go right ahead," he said with a sly sort of smile.

The guides had left base earlier to break trail to the campsite. I was supposed to join them with a pack mule loaded with supplies. It only took about a hundred yards to figure out why they'd left 'Black Beauty' behind, but by then it was too late. Between shuffling his hooves, stopping dead to snatch at grass, and completely ignoring my repeated, vigorous kicks, it was nearly dusk before we got there.

I never, ever tired of riding other horses, though. That's what made the permanent job, on an isolated guest ranch in the Nez Perce National Forest, so completely exciting. The place always had between 30 and 35 head of stock with new ones arriving every spring. Many of those were green-broke; owners sent them in to be "finished" over several months, which allowed the outfitter to save wear and tear on his own stock before fall hunting season. For a woman who'd grown up living, breathing, reading about, and completely absorbing herself in everything *horse*, this outranked being a kid in a candy store. Every time a fresh animal arrived I tried to be the first one on it. Some, like Bud, were more interesting than others.

"Spotty," who was part draft and part Appaloosa, was purchased for next to nothing (so bragged the ranch's foreman, who knew juuuuust enough about horses to be dangerous) as a mount for heavy riders. He was so thick-barreled I had to adjust my saddle cinch to get it around him. He was docile enough, but right away we crew members learned the foreman had been suckered.

Once we headed up the trail and Spotty began sweating, he smelled like a roomful of gym socks. "Stank" is the better word. In no time we were calling him "Stinky" instead of Spotty. The stench was so intense it was nearly impossible to draw a decent breath while on his back — plus he ambled along so lazily that nothing, not even the tap tap tap of a riding crop (I had an English saddle in addition to a Western) would speed him up. The minute we arrived at our high-mountain destination, I crouched by the lake to rinse his scent from my hands and face. To give Spotty credit, he was so placid that anyone could ride him. They never stopped complaining, though, about his drawback.

Underfed and half-hidden by a shaggy, unkempt coat, "Misty" was dropped off by a local rancher with instructions to "drag her into the woods, shoot her and leave her for bear bait." I couldn't figure out why he hated her so. Turned out Misty could run backwards with the speed of a cheetah if she felt threatened. And if that didn't work to dump a rider or two, she simply dropped to her knees, flopped over and rolled.

More than once she backed rump-first into a tree trunk yet kept on going, digging a trench at the base with her hind hooves. She wouldn't stop until her rider dismounted. After it happened half a dozen times I finally bought some spurs. She was the only horse or mule I ever used them on but *oh!* did they ever do the trick. The next time she backed into a tree and churned like a hamster on a wheel, I squeezed her with my legs (first) and then goosed her with the rowels. She paused briefly but dug in again. I goosed her harder. Instantly, her head flew up and she arched into the air in a perfect imitation of a gazelle, landing stiffly on all fours.

I nearly fell over backwards but somehow managed to stay seated. When we landed, though, I was jolted forward with so much force the back of her noggin connected directly with my nose. (It still has a scar on one side from where the sunglasses snapped in half.) But she never did it again. Eventually she blossomed into such a beauty, and became so easy to ride, that the same man who gave her away didn't recognize her when he stopped in months later to visit.

Some were just plain dangerous. Although "Ed" looked promising when he arrived from the sale yard — well-muscled, he was gruella with a thick, black mane — we couldn't leave him tied. He'd pull back and violently fight until the rope snapped and he flipped over. A sweet little white mare did a similar thing, only rearing, with a rider on. A small-boned brown mule often took the bit in his teeth and abruptly took off with his riders. A few others turned out to be vicious biters and kickers. The worst of them went right back where they'd come from; falling hard or getting hurt were not options when you lived in the middle of nowhere.

"Roscoe," a dun-colored mule, loved to trot downhill, which scared the hunters. A blood-bay mare we called "Killer" had gaits that were incredibly smooth, but she was so nasty they had to put a shock collar around her neck to keep her from chasing other horses from the hay manger. When she lunged at one of them — and the remote button was pushed — she slid to a stop so fast she slung dirt. (She wouldn't go near the manger after that. We had to carry a few flakes out to her at feeding time.)

Sister mules Kling and Klang, both chestnuts with Roman noses, constantly paced back and forth — even when tied. They were so addicted to it, they kept hunters awake at night in camp. The foreman tried putting hobbles on their front legs but it didn't do any good. They just took much smaller steps.

But when it came to winning the Most Aggravating prize, Guppy won hands-down. Originally named Goldie, he was an elegant, leggy Arab-cross with a honey-colored coat, white mane and tail, four matched white stockings, and a white stripe that ran from forehead to muzzle. With a comfortable, ground-covering trot and rocking chair canter, initially every crew member fought to use him, but the final reviews were not good.

"That dumbass has absolutely no sense of direction," one of the packers groused during a lunch break. "If I didn't rein him constantly he'd wander 'clear off the trail into the next county."

"You can't use him in a string, either," another agreed. "The idiot will stop short, stare into the distance and get his head jerked half-off by the mule in front of him. It happens *all* the time!"

Still another summed up his feelings while stretching across the table for the milk pitcher. "I think we should call him Goofy instead of Goldie. He has got to be one of the stupidest horses I've ever known! You can ride him by the same boulder ten times in a row and on the eleventh, he'll flip out, break the piggin' string, and run off!"

Simply because he was so stunning (and the ranch staff needed all the horses they could get that particular year), each of us started spending extra time with Goldie to help him settle down. We turned his head towards the things that scared him and gave him time to sniff them over thoroughly. (It didn't work. He still spooked when he felt like it.) We also taught him to ground-tie, which he took to very easily. But nothing stuck.

While riding him through the woods one afternoon with nine empty pack and saddle animals behind us, I noticed the last mule in the line had gotten one leg wrapped around a lead rope. The mule, Kasey, was awkwardly gimping on three legs with her head pulled down. Even though camp was less than 100 yards away, it had to be corrected.

I was glad to have chosen Goldie that day. Almost as tall as Spotty, he gave his rider a vantage point from which to see all the animals clearly. (A good packer practically rides sideways, constantly checking to make sure everything's okay: no saddles or packs are slipping; no sling ropes are dragging; no animals have broken loose; and no legs have been wrapped around lead ropes.) Dismounting and casually dropping Goldie's own lead rope on the ground — confident the regular, repeated training had been successful — I eased my way between myriads of tree trunks and lightly-blowing animals to reach the one that needed help.

And then, right about the time I'd freed Kasey's leg and was giving her a pat, Goldie decided he'd had enough of ground-tying. Casually, he started down the trail.

"Whoa!" I hollered out at him. He didn't flick an ear.

Maud, the horse behind him, followed obediently since her lead had been wrapped around the saddle horn. Sarge the mule followed Maude, then Rufus followed Sarge, and so on. Half-panicked, I dashed back the way I'd come, leaping over deadfall and ducking branches (ignoring the ones that scratched) as nimbly as an Indian. By the time I headed off Goldie, I was nearly out of breath.

"Whoa, whoa, whoa, you numbskull!" I panted, planting myself on the trail right in front of him and groping for the dragging lead. Goldie took one look at me and abruptly went into reverse, turning on the narrow trail with his hind legs frozen in place and shoving his body straight into the pack string. Maude followed (scraping her saddle against a trunk, which left deep marks in the leather), then Sarge, then Rufus and onward. "Whoa whoa *whoooooooaaaaaaaaa!*" I yelled again. Some of them stopped and some didn't. Bodies piled up against each other. Halter ropes wrapped around saddle rings. Heads got knocked together. Piggin' strings started snapping...and Goldie kept on walking at a steady pace towards home.

Again I ran to head him off, that time crashing and slamming through the trees. When I caught him, he slid to a stop and the horses and mules behind him crumpled together like dominoes. Another leg got caught under a lead rope. A head got pulled tight against a saddle horn. A butt swung out over the edge of the trail and the animal scrambled to regain its footing. Everywhere I looked there was a sea of horses and mules crammed together; it was what packers often ruefully referred to as a major wreck, and it was a doozy.

Goldie tried to swerve again but I jerked him around. "Dawgone you, knothead, what the %*_+:<# do you think you're doing?" I hollered. He tried to back up. The mare behind him grunted and backed into the one behind her. I cussed Goldie yet again, louder. Then with half my stock facing one direction and half facing another, one by one I untied each animal, led them (over more deadfall) to trees and tied them (Goldie, with non-slip knots), replaced broken piggin' strings, straightened saddles, and lined them out once again. Even though the fall air was cool, I was sweating putty balls by the time I climbed back into my saddle. "I'm going to kill you," I told him grimly. Focused on the campsite, he stepped out.

The hunters and guides, knowing someone was coming to drop off stock to haul them back to the lodge, were sitting on stumps around the fire pit when I rode in minutes later. "Here you go!" I called out cheerfully, passing Maude's lead rope to the first guide I saw. I'd lost time unravelling the wreck and was in a hurry to get back to the lodge. (At the very least, with his long legs Goldie would get me there fast.) It seemed strange how the men looked up at me with a mix of wariness and curiously, but I didn't think twice about it...until later.

I found out from Travis that the men — who up until that point only knew me to be sweet, friendly, and accommodating (a somewhat deceptive trait learned from Southern-born parents) — had heard every, single rotten word that I'd shouted at Goldie from the trail. "That lil' gal might act like she's wearing a hoopskirt," one remarked with a chuckle, "but apparently, there's bricks underneath it. Sounds like she'll throw 'em if she needs to!"

"She will," Travis had agreed solemnly. "Git outta her way."

When I held my face in my hands and groaned, Travis added quickly, "I think he admired your spunk." I didn't take my hands away from my face, so he added, "Don't worry about it! The hunters have certainly heard us guys yell at the livestock! It's okay!" But I was *a lot* more careful about what escaped my mouth after that embarrassing episode. At least, I made sure I was someplace where no one could hear me.

Since Goldie continued to be unpredictable no matter the situation and no matter who was handling him, his name soon morphed from Goldie to Goofy to McGoofy to McGuppy to Gup Head and Guppy. Frequently passed over now when it came to us choosing horses, he was taken to the sale yard that fall.

But just before we gave him up, he was enjoyed for real by a visitor named Patsy, who had grown up in a show ring. While her husband went out each day in search of elk, she took Guppy out into the meadow and played around with flying lead changes, figure eights, extended trots, and some basic dressage moves… really useful stuff in the backcountry. I hope he went to a good home, though. One that didn't have boogeymen.

Luckily, most of the horses and mules that passed through the ranch were both versatile and dependable. My favorite, Clay (I ended up buying him after Tee was retired) will forever remain the fastest that I've ever known. He was a rangy sorrel gelding that could accelerate from zero to thirty miles an hour in mere seconds if you needed serious speed. He was at his best when herds of free-ranging cattle wandered onto the property in search of the salt lick. Together we could round them up and push them out like nobody's business. On the other hand, he was so easy-going he'd settle down quick. I could trust him to mosey along home on loose reins while I relaxed.

Biscuit, a high-withered, strawberry roan mare also tore up roads like race tracks but she came with a bonus: she jumped like a steeplechaser. There was a tree down on the trail one day (a common occurrence) and instead of going around it I remember backing her up, getting a running start, and clearing it like she had wings.

Maple, a barrel-shaped Pinto, had such unusual patterns they turned her into a broodmare after just one season. She threw some amazing, tri-colored mule colts. Patsy, a Thoroughbred cross, delivered molly mules with legs so long it was unbelievable. Even my Tee J., who was retired at 24, managed to foal at the age of 25 thanks to a visiting Quarter horse stallion. (It was a complete and total surprise.) She presented me a dun filly, Bonnie, that was so gorgeous she stopped traffic after I moved from the ranch to McCall. But that's another story.

Ramblin' Rose, a red roan that was as slender as a greyhound, was so light-footed she literally skimmed on air. Leo, a gentle, dark brown Morgan, was as sturdy as an oak stump; we used him to drag logs into hunting camp. Mongo was completely bulletproof: you could fire from the saddle and he wouldn't move. We found this out by accident when an overly-zealous hunter saw a huge buck, yanked his rifle out of the scabbard and took a shot before his guide could stop him. The deer got away. Mongo just stood there. The guide was amazed. However, I don't think that poor gelding could hear very well afterwards.

But Jim, one of the Belgians that pulled the ranch's wagon, was my favorite ride of all. Late one fall when each camp was so busy every available animal was in use, I had no choice but deliver needed supplies on him. I had so many layers of clothes on against the snow and cold — and the stirrup was so high off the ground — that both Travis and Mark, who were heading out to different campsites, had to push on my boot bottoms to boost me into the saddle. Still it was a struggle to swing one leg across the over-loaded saddlebags.

"Wow, you'd better not try to dismount until you get there," Mark warned, staring up at me. He seemed very small. "You'll never get back on again."

"Don't worry," I grunted, "I'll wait!"

On Jim, who stood over 18 hands high, the whole world looked, felt and sounded different. He didn't just walk along the trail, he thundered. He didn't step or jump over deadfall, he crashed over top of it, crushing the bark with his wide, heavy hooves. And he put me 'way up high into the snow. The pack strings that had gone ahead of us had already knocked down what was on the lowest branches. But on Jim I hit fresh powder. I couldn't escape it no matter how often I ducked or leaned over one side. My face, gloves, and outback coat got completely covered. Snow even went down my shirt! But on the scale of one to ten, that ride sure was one of the best.

When I rode into camp I was grinning from ear to ear, and the first thing I heard was the snap of a camera. "I couldn't imagine what was coming towards us," the wide-eyed hunter exclaimed. "All I heard was this *boom boom boom* sound...and someone giggling."

He advanced the film and hurried over to assist me down. Awkwardly, still giggling, I managed to swing my right leg over Jim's broad rump but even with the hunter's arms protectively reaching upward to support me, I landed hard and my knees briefly buckled.

It was a long, long, *long* trip to the ground, but a delightful one.

*"Spotty peers through the lodge's picture window while Goldie grazes close-by."*

# CHAPTER 4

# WANNA BEES

(Shorter versions of this were printed in my *Fence Post* column,
"Living the good Life," as well as the March 2011 issue of *IDAHO
Magazine.* This is one of my favorite memories, and it has the details!)

The guest ranch was so remote a team and wagon hauled supplies and
people in and out. (In the winter we used snowmobiles.) There was a
lodge with an open-floor plan that included kitchen, pantry, dining
room, living room and bathroom. Under the staircase was a cellar with
so many shelves it held a year's supply of canned goods. On the second
floor were five "cubbies" with enough beds for fourteen people.

Additional buildings included a hay-storage barn, a chicken coop, a
tack room and corral, a shed, an outdoor shower, an outhouse, and an
A-frame that covered firewood. Later, a two-story cabin was added for
crew and any overflow guests. But for me, the most wonderful place in
the world was my own tiny cabin, built in 1896. Made of hand-hewn logs
(still stuffed with the original chinking) it had two teeny rooms down
and two rooms up, reached by a steep but sturdy staircase. The ceiling
was so low one could touch it, and the water that came from the faucets
was freezing cold. Woodstove heat seemed to go straight through the
walls, so in winter I slept under layers and layers of blankets. But I *loved*
that rustic hideaway — especially when it was completely illuminated
by the soft glow of candles and lanterns. With dozens set about on the
sink, shelves, nightstand, and desk there was more than enough light to
read or write by. (I had to be careful, though. One evening, when leaning

over to fetch another pen, one of my braids brushed a candle and briefly caught fire. The cabin stunk of burnt hair for a week.) From the upstairs office window, when sitting at the desk there was a wonderful view of the broodmare pasture. Downstairs, leaded glass panes looked out onto the yard, the split-rail fence that surrounded it, the 500-acre meadow, and a stretch of the wagon path that led through the woods to the trail head. There were no traffic noises, no street lights, no neighbors, and no stress-filled commutes.

Still, there was still plenty of excitement in the forms of guests, guides, and wranglers. I met all sorts of people. It was easy to pick out who the natural horsemen (and women) were as opposed to those who just dreamed about being cowboys. A favorite new hire (who didn't last a month) was eighteen-year old Dave from Chicago, who'd grown up on TV westerns. When asked how much riding experience he'd had, he scoffed "Tons!" Translating that to mean "none," the foreman assigned him an extra-slow and calm gelding named Gentle Ben.

Turned out, Dave had never sat on a horse in his life (outside a grocery store, maybe). During his first trip into the woods, everything Gentle Ben did caused Dave to panic — he couldn't even casually reach for a bite of grass without the kid yelling "Ho! Ho! Ho!"

Since Dave wouldn't take horse handling instructions from anyone, things only got worse for him. Throughout his time on the ranch, the rest of us sat back and snickered whenever his cap got knocked off by branches or he lost a stirrup or he got into a tight spot with a mule string. "Ho! Ho! Ho!" echoed through the woods on those occasions and in no time, Dave had earned the nickname "Santa." He wouldn't answer to it, though.

Twenty-five-year-old Peter from El Paso fibbed about his horsemanship skills, too, at least until the day he neglected to snug the cinch of his mule, Jessie, before mounting. Things were fine for the first half hour or so, but when a downhill trail got steep his gear started inching forward soooooooo gradually he wasn't even aware of it until he was sitting in the center of Jessie's neck. There was a creek crossing at the bottom and when Jessie stopped to take a drink, Peter went with him. Down. Up. Down. Up. The mule took several long drinks, casually raising his head and smacking his lips, oblivious of the rider who was struggling to stay balanced behind his ears. Pie-eyed and hollering for help (while the rest of us sat doubled over with laughter) Peter finally half-jumped and half-slid off to one side, belly-flopping into the water.

Pittsburgh-born Scott, who barely stood five feet two inches tall, claimed the tallest horse for his own right away. We watched, stifling snickers, as Scott tried and tried but couldn't get a foot into the stirrup. Irritably, he gave up and dragged the horse to a stump. Minneapolis Mike thought he was being clever by putting the reins between his teeth, like a John Wayne character, when he needed both hands to unzip his daypack. He nearly lost a few incisors when his horse stumbled. Charlie from Steubenville rode with his toes pointed so far out you could hang wet clothes on them. Al, from Des Moines, sat as loose as a sack of potatoes — which caused saddle sores on his poor animal. And even a camp cook hired for one season, Diana, had no clue how to saddle or bridle — regardless of her carefully cowgirl-constructed outfit of ponytail, Western shirt, bandana and store-bought belt buckle.

Some boys tried harder than others to be horsemen. At least they took instruction from a female. Craig, from small town Wisconsin, was one of them. But I doubt any witnesses will ever forget the wild ride he took on my personal Quarter horse, Clay.

It happened a few years after I'd moved to the ranch. Frequently, loose cattle turned out to graze in the surrounding forest wandered onto the property in search of the salt block. Clay and I could herd them back where they belonged single-handedly; he was quick, cow-savvy, and so "push-button" it was like dancing with the perfect partner. Squeeze him lightly and he increased speed accordingly. Touch one rein and he'd turn on a dime. Duck alongside his neck and he'd pick his way under branches with barely a nick. Sit back in the saddle and he'd slide to a stop. But the thing he was best at was going from zero to *blaze* with a simple trick I'd learned from the movie, "Man from Snowy River." All you had to do was make a hissing sound.

One morning when the ranch was crammed with guests and I was hustling about the kitchen fixing breakfast, cattle were spotted at the edge of the meadow. The crew quickly gathered some horses and saddled to go after them. I wanted to join in the fun but couldn't; there was too much to do.

The lodge's screen door banged and boots clomped across the floor while I was turning bacon on the wood stove. "Carolyn, can I take Clay?" Craig called out, breathless with anticipation.

Craig was what they called a dude hire — someone right out of guide school who hadn't yet gotten his license. Mostly, he split and chopped firewood in addition to other odd chores. "Please? Can I take Clay?" he repeated, clumsily blocking my way as I moved towards the counter. I can still see him standing before me in his brand-new cowboy hat with the stampede straps pulled tight under his chin. He was lanky, about 6'2", with large brown eyes framed by roundish, John Denver-style, gold-rimmed glasses. There were pimples on his chin.

"No way," I said immediately. "He's too high-powered…."

"Pleeeeeaaaaassssssseee?" He begged, clasping both hands together. "He came up to the corral with the other horses. He's just standing there! We need him! He's the best!" When I hesitated, focused on breaking eggs into a bowl, he persisted. "C'mon! I know I can handle him! I've ridden lots of the horses here already and you said I was improving! C'mon! I *know* I can do it. Pleeeeeaaaaaasssssseee?"

Looking down, whipping the eggs with a whisk, I stifled a smile. It was no secret Craig was sweet on a dark-haired teen girl who was visiting with her family. Along with the other guests, they had gathered at the corral with their coffee mugs to watch as the crew prepared to go. This would be his turn to shine. Feeling a bit like I was handing Ferrari keys over to a newly-licensed driver, I finally stopped, looked up, and sighed, "Well, all right."

The kid gave a brief fist-pump, burst out with "Yes!" and abruptly turned to leave but I grabbed for his sleeve. "Whoa, boy," I warned. "Be careful. Ease the cattle out, don't push them. You can trot and canter but don't run. Clay might well jump out from underneath you."

Craig nodded but I know he barely heard me. He bolted toward the screen door and let it bang again. I winced and returned to the wood stove, occasionally glancing out the wide picture window to watch them going by. They never did.

For ten minutes I restlessly wandered back and forth, sometimes with one hand cupped under dripping utensils. Suddenly, there came the sound of running footsteps.

The door flew open again and the rest of the crew members literally fell onto the linoleum, howling like hyenas. One went to his knees, holding his stomach. The others leaned on the walls or each other for support. The noise was practically deafening. "What on earth happened?" I asked, nervously wiping both hands on my apron, hurrying over and bracing myself for the worst. It took a while, but one finally managed to gasp out the story.

With every guest lined elbow-to-elbow at the railings — some with cameras poised — Craig had stepped up onto Clay and gallantly tipped his hat in the direction of his teen crush. She had beamed back. Then, simply because he'd heard me do it, he hissed.

The gelding, which had been standing quietly before the open gate, dug in and took off from a standstill. So powerful was the motion of his hindquarters that Craig instantly lost his balance, dropped the reins, and slid behind the saddle. Downhill towards the meadow Clay flew, ears back and tail level with his spine. "And there was Craig with a death-grip on the cantle," one of the guys hooted, straightening and wiping at his eyes, "yell...yelling..." he paused to laugh again, "*whooooooaaaaaaaaaa* all the way until we heard him thud as he hit the ground!"

When Craig finally showed up at breakfast, he had grass stains on one side of his shirt and jeans and his glasses were bent. Guides and guests hunkered down and gave each other subtle grins as they passed the platters, milk and pancake syrup towards him. The conversations renewed, but no one spoke to him. We could see he was deflated.

I briefly touched Craig's shoulder when I poured his coffee. Images of my own past, spectacular falls came to mind while moving around the table, refilling other mugs. There had been plenty. When Craig forlornly followed the rest of the crew out after breakfast, I caught his arm again. "It's okay," I whispered. "Every good horseman hits the ground along the way." His large brown eyes settled on mine and he smiled a little. Ever so slightly, in the manner of a cowboy, he lifted his chin in acknowledgement while settling his hat down on his head — this time with the stampede straps in back.

*"Clay, the gelding that took Craig on his wild ride."*

# CHAPTER 5

# WOODS WORKING

(A version of this story appeared in the November 2016 issue of *IDAHO Magazine*.)

Hunting season was finally over on the ranch. I'd been up by three o'clock nearly every morning for three-and-a-half months, not collapsing into bed until after ten pm, and was completely and totally exhausted.

Just a few days earlier I'd cooked a huge tray of lasagna, four loaves of French bread, cinnamon-spiced applesauce, and fresh-made cottage cheese (thanks to Rosie, the ranch cow). Fourteen people devoured the meal in under twenty minutes. Most left the following morning, travelling three miles through the forest on horseback to the trailhead, where their trucks were parked. I breathed a sigh of relief as the last mule in the pack string disappeared into the trees. The snow had reached halfway to their knees.

The final guest, a man named Flynn, moved about his room upstairs whistling softly as he packed. Clutching a third cup of coffee, I watched snow falling out the dining room window. Some time that afternoon, a pilot from Arnold's Aviation in Cascade was due in to fetch Flynn, his gear and the elk he'd shot.

I couldn't wait. I wanted *everyone* gone.

At times hunters drove me crazy. Far from the watchful eyes of their wives, men guzzled the beer and spirits they'd brought (which made them talk louder), smoked cigars, and used clean bathroom towels to wipe unwashed hands on. They set coffee cups on the piano and spread gun-cleaning tools out on the coffee table. The seriously overweight ones gobbled forbidden foods like fried pork chops and gravy, regardless of doctor's warnings. "Good thing my surgeon can't see this," one of them observed while liberally dumping salt on his mashed potatoes. "He'd warn me not to do it."

"Well, he's not here, is he?" his companion countered jovially, helping himself to a second piece of pie.

A 63-year-old named Dick actually *needed* a doctor one evening after hiking, sweating, and over-indulging all day. Pushing himself back from the dinner table, he set down his napkin, rubbed his tummy, said good-night…and abruptly fell over backwards, hitting the floor with a thud.

"Call 911!" one of his buddies yelled.

"We don't have a phone," I responded sharply, bolting to the sink. Returning with a dampened washrag, I knelt beside the unconscious man and draped it over his forehead. "Dick. Dick! Are you ok? Talk to me," I pleaded, lightly slapping at his wrists.

"Call 911!" the buddy repeated, turning in circles.

"There's no phone here!" Several others shouted in unison.

Dick stirred. "What happened?" He groaned.

"Do you feel clammy?" the foreman asked, kneeling on his other side.

"What? Huh? Hey, I'm okay. Really." Dick struggled to rise.

"Get him to the couch," someone said. At least four pairs of arms reached out to assist. I set blankets out and we gingerly laid him down. Volunteers took shifts throughout the night, alternately bringing the patient fresh water, rotating damp towels, and asking him how many fingers were being held up. He rested quietly. To keep things calm (me, especially) I placed a few extra kerosene lanterns close to the music books and began playing the piano. Discreetly peeking around the room at 2:00 am, I noticed with relief that sprawled in various armchairs, he and the volunteers were finally sleeping.

Even if Dick had been actively dying there was nothing we could do. The hangar at Arnold's Aviation didn't open until 6:00 am. Only then was it possible to call out on the radio-phone to have them relay messages over a landline. (No one was at Arnold's after dark; Ray, the owner, and his wife, Carol, went home.) But Dick not only improved, he rose, showered, and ate yet another greasy, hearty breakfast. "Thanks for playing last night," he said. "It sounded like angels from Heaven."

And despite our numerous pleas, he insisted on scouting with his guide, Travis, that very afternoon. "If I'm going to have a heart attack and die, I'm gonna do it in the woods," he said cheerfully.

Behind Dick's back, with copper hair sticking out from both sides of his wool cap, Travis looked at me and deadpanned, "It's okay. I'll drag him home."

There's nothing like being completely isolated, surrounded by one's peers, to bring out the most macho, carefree and primitive behaviors in most males. With no on-demand hot water, some stopped shaving, changing their clothes, brushing their teeth, and yes, even bathing. Without a Mrs. around to monitor them, they peppered their stories with expletives, challenged each other to arm-wrestling matches at the dining room table (more than once knocking off entire boxes of toothpicks), or tracked mud across newly-mopped floors. Sitting around the fire pit in camp, forgetting there was a female nearby in the cook tent, they openly burped, passed gas, and told jokes that were so filthy — and totally hilarious — that I had to cram a towel against my mouth so they wouldn't hear the laughter.

I shared what I'd heard with my sister, Nancy, who flew from Ohio each year to cook for a month. Stationed at campsites about two miles apart, we either walked or rode horses back and forth every third day for visits. "Yoooo hoooo!" she called out to let me know she was approaching.

"Step into my office," I'd say in response, holding back a tent flap, "I have *the best* joke to tell you!"

One of the rowdiest groups consisted of four brothers from New Jersey who played poker each night after supper was cleared. Growing louder and more enthusiastic with each game, they lunged at each other, slammed down their cards, and vigorously argued (especially over whose turn it was to run to the creek for more beer). At bedtime, I literally had to scoop up the cards and shove the players out of the cook tent before tightly lacing the canvas flaps, washing my face in a dish tub, and crawling into my sleeping bag — after carefully checking it first for things that didn't belong there. (I'm not the first person to be startled by a rubber snake or spider.)

Hunters poured ice-cold water over the heads of companions who were trying to shower. They crept up behind outhouses and yanked makeshift doors open while someone (luckily, never me) was sitting inside. They hid each other's reading glasses, watches, or dentures, or took wet boots from under the woodstove and placed them outside. A shout followed by raucous laughter, concluding with one man chasing another through the forest, indicated yet another prank had been successfully accomplished.

On the other hand, some guys were real pains, like the one who insisted on stopping frequently to dump talcum powder down his shirt and pants to prevent chafing. He didn't listen when warned the scent would be picked up by wild game. He never saw anything, either, and so left the ranch mad. Or the one who arrived in camp only to realize he'd forgotten his favorite pillow at the lodge. He begged me to fetch it. I rode four hours, total, but then he wouldn't use it. He said it smelled like sweat. There were hunters who claimed they knew how to ride but couldn't, or who said they had practiced with their rifles but hadn't. Some brought brand-new boots that weren't broken in, resulting in wicked blisters. (They blamed the guides for walking them too far.) Some even forgot to pack their licenses! But worst was the one who fired at an animal without taking careful aim.

The sun was getting low one October when Pat, known for his short and direct sentences, cracked open the back door of the lodge and grunted, "Where's th' foreman?"

"I don't know. Maybe up by the corral?" I answered, leaning over the kitchen counter. "What's wrong?"

"Hunter made a gut-shot." Abruptly, the door closed.

Pat had spent an hour bugling the elk in. His hunter got impatient, however, and when the animal hesitated 50 yards away and turned to run, he fired blindly. The bull took off.

They picked up a sparse blood trail and followed it until the sun got low and Pat decided to fetch help. Armed with flashlights, a mounted search party headed out to see if they could find the slow-bleeding animal. The men tracked that elk all the way to the Montana Road, a long, heavily-rutted dirt stretch that was a favorite with from-the-truck hunters. They found the elk — or what was left — just as the moon rose.

Someone had finished the poor animal off, dumped the gut pile, tossed the meat into their pickup bed, and used blood to write 'THANKS' in the snow.

"It's okay," Pat's hunter said shortly after the group had trudged in after midnight. "We'll find another bull."

Bleary-eyed Pat, picking at his reheated dinner, turned his head so slowly that one barely saw it move. But I witnessed the wordless snarl.

Mark had an unfortunate experience, as well. Since he was one of the most animated and enthusiastic guides I'd ever worked with, I knew something was wrong when he entered the lodge one afternoon and didn't say a word. Simultaneously, his hunter, Floyd, trudged slowly upstairs with downcast eyes, still wearing his hat and coat with a rifle slung over one shoulder.

"There I was," Mark explained later in the privacy of the guide's cabin, "bugling my brains out with this bull back and forth, back and forth, trying to draw him in. We started at sun rise. Man, it was so cool! He'd come closer, then circle to the left or the right, then either bugle right on top of me or stay silent for five or ten minutes. Once, he was quiet for so long we thought he'd wandered off but I just *knew* I was bringing him in! I just *knew* we were going to get him!"

It wasn't easy to imitate the shrill, rising call of a bull elk. The guys practiced constantly with tiny, colored diaphragms which fit against the roof of the mouth (often accidentally spitting them out). Adjusting the outtake of air, they made squeaking noises at first, then little chirps, and then, with just the right amount of exhalation came a long, drawn-out imitation bugle. To make the bugles louder, to travel longer distances, the guys blew into flexible tubes.

Around eleven, Floyd had sat down on a fallen log to eat. Mark continued, "The bull made up his mind to come get me. He was grunting and snorting and raking his anglers against trees and thrashing his head...*man*, he was mad! We could smell him from a long way away because he kept stopping to paw at the ground and piss on himself!"

Mark's blue eyes grew wider and his hands waved more wildly as his story reached the climax. "Seriously, I could feel the ground shaking! By then I was getting hoarse because my throat was so sore, but I kept going, and he kept coming until I finally gestured at Floyd to get his gun ready. But that numbskull sat there chewing until the bull actually came into view."

The moment Mark glimpsed the dark muzzle and golden-brown hide through the underbrush and pines, he knew they had a monster. "When the bull trotted into the clearing with his head back and I saw the antlers? Good grief, I almost passed out!" He held both arms out as far as they could go, adding, "He was *huuuuuuuuge*!"

All of us staffers leaned forward, pie-eyed with anticipation as we waited to find out what happened next. "And right then," Mark spat out in disgust, "Floyd reached for his rifle while he's crumpling up a *#*%^*_> candy wrapper!" The bull, of course, abruptly disappeared.

Yet as we slumped back in our chairs, stunned at his misfortune, Mark added with wonder, "How is it that an 800-pound animal can suddenly tip-toe over deadfall without making a sound?" It was one of those gifts of Mother Nature that made hunting what it really was…a thrill in the midst of defeat.

Only a small percentage of the people who came to hunt truly knew what they were doing and what they were in for: steep terrain, thin air, thick trees, heavy deadfall, and wildlife that blended in perfectly with their surroundings. They had water-proof boots that were well worn, and duffle bags filled with wool clothing (instead of denim or any other material that made noise). They practiced frequently with their bows, muzzleloaders, or rifles at home, and they practiced again shortly after arriving at the ranch. They wore no aftershave, cologne, or underarm deodorant on the days they were heading out to hunt, and they were in great physical shape.

For some of them, knowledge, skill, good weather, and patience paid off. Tom, an Illinois hog farmer with four daughters, spent fifteen years saving up for his trip. He had plenty of whitetail racks, but he wanted an elk. On day four he bagged a 6x6 bull with a rack so wide a small extension had to be built onto his house before the mount could be displayed. A card arrived a year later containing a picture of it, along with a note that said, "Five daughters now."

Dave, a professional knife sharpener, shot a blond-colored black bear. His friend Larry, a carpenter, got a black one the next day. John, a retired policeman, shot a mule deer buck with an impressive, atypical rack. Some seasons, it seemed like every time we turned around a packer was being summoned to fetch yet another carcass.

Understandably, those sportsmen were mighty proud of what they'd shot and were eager to help load it. A bear could be carried by one mule, but it took two for an extra-stout buck. (The first mule got the front quarters, the heart, and the liver. The second got the hindquarters and antlers.) And a bull elk was a three-animal job. One carried the front quarters; a second, the hind quarters; and a third, the heart, liver, rack and hide. (Most men wanted the hide left in one piece, so it could be tanned and displayed). Thankfully for me, the mules on the ranch were on the small side, which made loading much easier.

It still took effort, though. After an especially heavy quarter was heaved up against the packsaddle, one person braced it against his or her shoulder while another tied it on. If a third person was available, he stood on the opposite side and gripped the rings of the packsaddle so it wouldn't slide. He then hurried around and supported that first quarter while the second was being strapped on.

Packers had to constantly check each animal in the string as they wound along the trails. If saddle rings started shifting too far to one side it was time to stop, adjust, rebalance, or tighten. No packer wanted a load to roll. It meant completely untying everything, resetting the saddle and pad, and starting over — which isn't easy when you're alone, tired, cold, or in the dark.

There was lots of celebration after success. Dirty, bloody and deliriously happy, with their meat wrapped in game bags, hanging high, men pulled logs close to the fire pit and told their stories over and over. If staying at the lodge, they regaled everyone around the dining room table. I have many fond memories of those times even though the names and faces aren't so clear anymore. But there's one man I'll *never* forget.

His name was James, and I believe he was 6'8" tall and weighed 340 pounds. His group was from Cleveland and they'd booked a week at the lodge. But after a drop camp opened unexpectedly, the guys voted to spend a night out just for the experience. James, however, was reluctant to go. "I'm fine here," he said from the living room, where he took up nearly half a couch.

His friends were insistent. "C'mon! It'll be fun!"

"No. No, I'd rather stay." He kept shaking his head. No amount of reasoning persuaded him.

Turned out James was afraid of hurting one of the ranch's average-sized horses. After a hurried, whispered conference, Travis, Mark and I fetched Big Jim the Belgian. We adjusted the widest saddle to fit him, attached regular reins (the longest pair we had) to his snaffle bit, and led Big Jim to the steps of the lodge.

James was thrilled. Immediately, he began referring to himself as "Large James" so the pair "wouldn't get confused with each other." And after returning from camp, he relayed, "I was watching the other horses going along the trail ahead of us and noticed that each one kind of skipped over fallen logs. Not my Big Jim, though! He blazed through 'em just like a bulldozer!" Large James held both hands out, fingers spread, to mimic Big Jim's enormous hooves. He was lit up like a lighthouse. I knew exactly how he felt.

Large James' face came to mind that last morning of hunting season as I watched the falling snow flakes. It was one thing to ride a horse or lead a string through deepening snow, but landing a plane in it was much, much trickier. I started to worry. If the accumulation grew too high, the wheels of the Cessna could bog down and it might get stuck.

A voice crackled through the radio phone with the ranch's call numbers, and I jumped. It was Carol Arnold from the Cascade hangar.

I picked up the mic and responded, "374."

"Ray will be in as soon as the weather clears to get that hunter and his elk," she said. "He needs to know how many inches you have on the airstrip."

"We'll measure and call you back. Thanks! 374 out."

"371."

Carol's husband, Ray, had been flying for nearly two decades. If anyone could get in or out, it was him, but still the next several hours were nerve-wracking. The foreman fired up a snowmobile and sped off to check accumulation: it was 14 inches. When a pocket of blue sky finally opened around 3:00. Carol radioed again to tell us Ray was on his way, but, as she warned, "we only have a short window of time to get your guest from the ranch to Boise before dark."

"He'll be ready," I assured her.

Flynn laced his boots, double-checked for his wallet, hotel reservation, and airline tickets, went upstairs to make sure nothing had been left behind, and took one last walk around the yard for more pictures. We stood on the porch and made small talk. I didn't have my coat on and was shivering. When the roar of the Cessna was finally heard over the mountains, I gave him a brief hug goodbye before ducking back inside. He climbed behind the foreman on the snowmobile and I watched from the window as they took off through the opened gate, dragging a sled that was loaded with luggage, elk meat, and antlers.

Exhaling deeply, I sank onto the couch. For a moment, I didn't know what else to do. Nearly three weeks would pass, depending on snow pack, before guests started showing up on their own snowmobiles for day trips. Most of the crew has gone home for the holidays. After all this time, my life was my own again, and relief slowly flowed through my veins. *I was free*!

No more beds to make! No more mud to clean up! No more endless meals to plan, dishes to wash, questions to answer, or shelves to dust! I could nap in the rocking chair every afternoon! Read a book! Practice sewing on the treadle! Learn new songs on the piano! Write all the letters I wanted, whenever I wanted. *Yeeeeeeessssssssssss*! Removing my apron, I tossed it over a chair and did a reckless impromptu dance around the floor.

The Cessna fired up and the engine rumbled, the roar rising and falling as Ray turned on the circular roundabout. It stopped for a moment; the red stripe stood out against the green, white, and blue background. Then, spitting snow behind three wheels, the plane started accelerating down the 1800-foot airstrip, gaining speed for take-off. It was always exciting to watch Ray fly, so I returned to the window.

Then abruptly, out of sight at the far end of the strip, the Cessna aborted.

I watched with my nose pressed against the frosted glass, stifling a rising sense of alarm as the foreman shot down the wide expanse after them. Pines blocked the view, so I stood on my tiptoes. Nothing happened for the longest time.

Then...the snowmobile reappeared...and it was carrying...no...was it? No. *No*! Not one but two forms. Exhaust billowed behind the machine in a long, foggy cloud as it headed straight to the lodge. I stepped onto the porch right in time to see Flynn dismounting. Without lifting the shield of his helmet to speak, the foreman continued onward to park the machine in the shed. "Wh...what happened?" I asked anxiously.

"There was too much weight to get off the ground," Flynn replied.

Dreading to hear the answer, I pressed him. "Too...much weight?"

Sheepishly, he nodded. "Ray's dropping my stuff at the hangar tonight. He'll be back for me in the morning."

*"Most of the hunters were lots of fun to be around."*

# CHAPTER 6

# MAIL CALL

(A version of this appeared in the April
2017 issue of *IDAHO* magazine.)

The snow was thigh-high and each step was a struggle. Pausing to catch my breath I muttered, "Okay, I give up. Where'd you drop it, Ray?" Half-blinded by late morning sunshine, I rotated slowly. As far as the eye could see there was nothing but snow-covered meadow, bright blue sky with puffy white clouds, snow-capped mountains, and thousands upon thousands of pine trees. About 100 yards away, smoke curled from both chimneys of the lodge. Up the hill by the barn, thirty-three horses and mules nibbled at their morning hay.

But there was absolutely no sign of the waterproofed, orange nylon, USPS Mail bag. Tossed out of the plane's window maybe an hour earlier, it had sunk completely out of sight. Rubbing a hand across my forehead, I sighed.

Mail day is more priceless than gold when you live in the rugged, remote Idaho backcountry. The isolated ranches scattered along the Salmon River, as well as the three which had been built high in the mountains — including the one I lived on — received deliveries just once a week during summer and fall. Besides mail, Ray flew in groceries, gardening tools, saddles, liquor, canvas tents, jet boat parts, fencing material, chickens, dogs, llamas, or whatever else the year-round residents needed. If it fit into his single-engine Cessna 206 airplane (and didn't go over the weight limit), he would do it.

An hour or so before Ray's expected arrival we shooed stray horses and mules off the airstrip. The windsock was checked to make sure it hadn't wrapped around its pole. Guests gathered on the porch, laughing and talking, because *everyone* wanted to witness the sight of a plane landing on a grass airstrip in the middle of nowhere.

Some of the remote airstrips were real doozies. (Ray took me and a college classmate, Katie, along on the route one day so we've had personal, stomach-twisting experience.) One was so deep in a canyon he had to do half a dozen circles, dropping closer and closer to the strip with each pass, before we could land. Another required a 45-degree ascent to a postage stamp-sized landing field. Still others had been smoothed out on knolls above the water.

Compared to them, our ranch's high-altitude airstrip was easy (or so Ray said, but I think he was kidding). At least it was flat and fairly long. We used a gas-powered mower to cut the grass, which prevented the plane's wheels from dragging. It was the most boring job in the world to go back and forth, back and forth about a hundred times in the hot summer sun, but we understood how important the chore was and took turns.

Anyhow, it was about the only chance I ever had for wearing shorts, trying to get a tan.

Working in the lodge on mail day I kept a close ear to the radio phone, a battery-powered, CB-type unit which had been rigged in a corner of the kitchen and ran off a solar-powered battery. It crackled with voices from the ranches along the Salmon as they called the hangar to report Ray's whereabouts. Depending on his loads, he took more time at some places than others. If there was a cake or fresh-baked bread, he tended to stay longer.

The sound of his engine firing up could be heard as he left the ranch closest to ours, even though it was 20 miles away by road. As the humming sound grew closer and closer, necks craned as each person tried to catch the first glimpse of him topping the mountains. "There he is!" came the shout and as one, the guests and crew rose, headed down the stairs and across the yard, opened and closed the gate, passed the garbage-burning pit, and strolled across the meadow to the airstrip. Once, wearing an apron, T-shirt, and blue jeans, I was challenged to a spontaneous foot race by three kids who were in for vacation. With the plane taxiing down the airstrip towards the turnabout, I bolted like a rocket at GO! (It wasn't much different from running a High school 100-yard dash except I had no tennis shoes.) The kids were beaten soundly, and as we clomped onto the porch ten minutes later, their father (who had a large black video camera balanced on one shoulder) glanced down at my feet. "You ran *that fast* in cowboy boots?" he asked incredulously.

"Yup. Sure did."

"You're kidding!"

"Try going for a week without mail and see how fast you can run," I replied seriously, using one elbow to open the door latch since both arms were completely wrapped around the bag.

Once untied and inverted over the dining room picnic table, the mail bag often disgorged so many envelopes, magazines, packages, flyers, boxes and newspapers that some tumbled to the floor. All of us eagerly bent over them, heads touching and hands moving quickly as we sorted for anything bearing our names. "My sister had her baby!" or "I got the long johns I ordered!" or "I finally have some pictures from my girlfriend!" might be heard after the rapid-fire tearing of papers.

Most important were those letters, which were carried off to be read and re-read from porch chairs, benches, and couches. Letters from home. Letters from friends. Letters with news that, although a little outdated, was still fresh to us. Sitting at dinner over the nights that followed, we shared important tidbits over and over because we had to make them last.

After dinner on mail day, I could barely wait to wipe down the table, push the benches in, sweep the floor, shut off the propane lights and retreat to the quiet of my cabin. Lester, my Siamese-mix (and later, twin tabbies Squirrel and Monroe), always lingered on the back porch and followed as I walked across the yard. Inside, after brushing my teeth and scaling the steep, narrow wooden stairs to my bedroom I lit half a dozen candles and antique kerosene lanterns at the desk, pulled out fresh paper and a pen, and wrote responses to letters until my wrist began hurting.

There was a knack to writing without electricity. The wick of a lantern, if turned to high, blackened the globe. If too low, it flickered and went out. And it had to be trimmed regularly for the flame to give even, steady light. With candles, one learned not to sneeze without covering the mouth; otherwise, drops of wax blew all over. Also, flies and moths were drawn to open flames. Sometimes they kamikazed right through the fire and flopped about on the desk, mortally wounded, until I finished them off.

Daily, I added more and more paragraphs and descriptions to each letter like one might with a diary. They couldn't be picked up until either Ray returned or someone on the crew made the day-long trip to Grangeville for supplies (and a post office drop). Patience was a virtue developed by necessity.

Although we got weekly deliveries in good weather, over the winters Ray delivered only on the first and third Wednesdays of each month. He landed on skis, handed us the bag, and visited for ten or fifteen minutes (sharing backcountry gossip) before taking off with the outgoing mail. To make it as easy as possible for him, we kept the airstrip packed smooth as glass, regularly running over it with snowmobiles. But when one lives in an area that gets between 160 and 200 inches of snow accumulation each season, it's impossible to keep up. When it became unsafe Ray threw the bag out of his window.

This worked fine as long as one knew he was coming. Flying low, his toss was so accurate the faded orange bag landed within twenty yards of my feet. Sometimes, if the snow surface was especially icy, it practically slid right to me. But if the Arnold's Aviation schedule got switched around, as it happened on that long, frustrating morning...well, I got caught off-guard. What made it especially frustrating was, that month had had five Wednesdays, which meant no mail had been received in *three* weeks. And with several 40-degree afternoons in a row, softening the snow, the over-loaded bag had sunk deep. *Really* deep.

Totally oblivious on that sunny spring morning, I'd suited up and broken trail to the woodshed, loaded the wheelbarrow half a dozen times, and pushed it to and from the lodge and my cabin to refill the wood boxes. I'd broken trail uphill to the barn with Lester, Squirrel, and Monroe behind me. (The snow was so deep all that could be seen were the top inches of their tails.) I'd played String with them, using leftover twine after tossing hay out to the horses and mules.

Grabbing an axe, I'd scaled the fence, eased down the slick hillside, and used it to break thin ice in the creek for the livestock. I'd milked Rosie, the ranch cow, poured some out for the cats, hogs, and chickens, checked the coop for random eggs, and gathered assorted debris that lay scattered about the yard. Returning to the lodge, I'd unlaced my sturdy winter boots, set them by the barrel stove, added a few logs to it, tossed my hat and gloves to the side, unzipped my heavy jacket, and hung it on a peg to drip dry. Judging from the soft clicks and pops coming from the other side of the room I knew that Maggie, the cook stove, needed more wood as well. After refilling her grate, I put on an apron, strained warm milk through a cheesecloth into a glass gallon jar, opened the kitchen window, and shoved it in the snowbank to cool. Then I set about fixing lunch for the fellas, who had said they'd return from a scouting trip around 1:00 because they wanted to be there when the mail arrived.

I filled a large pot with water and set it on Maggie's hottest burner to start a soup. Inside the pantry, I held the apron by both corners, made a pouch and filled it with onions, potatoes, and carrots. I was shifting other cans around, looking for garlic powder when...far off in the distance... there came a distant, low humming sound, as unmistakable as a giant swarm of bees in a flowering cherry orchard.

'No. It can't be,' I thought to myself. 'Ray's not due until two or three.' But the Cessna's engine had its own distinctive roar. Backing out of the pantry, I froze and focused. Without a doubt, an airplane was approaching — and *fast*, from an entirely different direction than what I was used to.

I lunged for the kitchen counter, stood on my tip-toes, dumped the contents of the apron, shot across the linoleum floor and dove for my boots, skipping the grommets and wrapping the long laces around my calves. The laces got intertwined so when I stood and tried to run, I fell over. Then, right as I was flopping around on the floor frantically trying to untangle myself, Ray flew over.

The Cessna's shadow floated eerily over the lodge's rooftop and porch, briefly blocking the sun. Out the dining room picture window came a glimpse of white underbelly, wheels, and a red-striped tail. The engine sound dropped as the Cessna cleared the fence and the trees around the salt lick before coasting across the meadow. Then abruptly, as Ray powered upward to clear the mountaintops, it roared loud enough to rattle the panes. And over that retreating roar came my own, panicked wail: "*Noooooooooooooooooooooooo!!*"

Kicking off the boots, I skidded to the window and stared, searching for signs of orange. Binoculars were on the sill and I grabbed them, scanning carefully. Nothing. Scowling, I headed for the chair by the radio phone, plopped down, and listened to see if anyone else was on air. Things were quiet, so I picked up the mic and said, "371 this is 374."

"371," Carol answered cheerfully, her voice a little crackly from the static.

"Um, Ray was just here. I wasn't expecting him so don't know where he dropped the mail bag. Any ideas?"

There was a moment of dead air. "Sorry, I tried to patch through to you earlier," she replied. "Something came up and he had to switch the route. Your place was first today."

'No kidding,' I thought sullenly. When I didn't respond right away, Carol added, "Let me try to reach him in the air."

Standing on the chair I scanned some more, hoping the bag would be visible from a different angle. A few of the mules ambled downhill along the fence line towards the creek to get water. Frost covered their manes, which had been shaved during hunting season and now stood up in spikes.

Carol came back on. "374, this is 371."

"I'm here."

"He said it's at the southwest corner of the bridge close to the grove of Aspens."

"Great!" I replied. "374 out."

"371." Carol cleared the radio for other mail day callers.

I hustled upstairs with the binoculars. For at least ten minutes I scoured the suggested area, stopping several times to adjust focus. The sparkling snow was almost painful to look at, and whenever I took breaks (closing both eyes) that whiteness lingered inside my head for a while. But there was no orange mound. Groaning, I trudged past the lodge's guest bedrooms – each cubby divided by high bookshelves – and went back down the stairs. I put my gear on and went outside. The further I got from the lodge, the deeper and more difficult the snow drifts became but onward I struggled, soundly cursing the boys for taking all the snowmobiles. As far as I was concerned, they were just taking joyrides.

My knees rose and fell awkwardly and both arms alternately flung sideways as I tried to stay upright. For the better part of an hour I flopped between bridge, trees, meadow, and creek getting more and more frustrated by the minute. By the time I gave up, my jeans were soaked, the snow had worked its way over the tops of both boots, and my entire left side was damp from where I'd lost balance and lurched over.

Back at the lodge, I headed straight for the radio phone, not caring if I tracked across the floor. "371 this is 374." That time I *knew* I sounded frustrated.

Carol came back on air. "371."

"I'm sorry, but I simply can't find the bag. I've looked everywhere."

The dead air space was much longer than before, and my mind raced. I figured that at least two dozen people within listening range were by now glued to their own radio-phones, listening intently. In the backcountry, everyone knew everyone else's business because it was like being on a telephone party line. Inwardly I cringed, thinking that most residents, by that point, had decided I was completely and totally blind.

Finally, Carol came back on. "I'll radio him again," she assured me.

I stood, craning my neck once again to look out the window while fighting tears of impatience. *Where was it?* Our letters were getting wet! The ink would run and we wouldn't be able to read them! For once, I wished we had a mailbox and a man in a uniform, driving a white and blue truck, driving right to the curbside.

After what seemed like forever, Carol returned. "He says he'll fly back over and show you."

I knew right away it meant a lot of time and gas for them and was instantly grateful. "Great! Thanks so very much!" I responded, relieved. "I'll wait outside."

One of the benches on the porch was getting full sun and I sat on it, turning my face to the warmth. Lester, who had been dozing upright in a bright spot against the lodge, picked his way along the dry spots under the eaves and climbed into my lap. Aside from his purring there was no sound in the Idaho backcountry beyond a gentle breeze. The pines swayed, and from those closest came the familiar sounds of creaking. Closing my eyes and stroking Lester's fur, I relaxed and listened.

I adored that gentle creaking sound. While in guide school I'd often climbed the hill behind base camp and sat on a large boulder to be alone to read or write, stopping often to watch those long, slender trees do their graceful movements. Sometimes I climbed so high above base camp the tents, the plastic-covered outhouse, the corral, and the trucks appeared no bigger than matchboxes. Once I was completely surprised by a buck which stood staring from barely twenty feet away. He blended in so perfectly with the forest I looked right through him at first.

How often I had written to the people I loved back then, sharing the details of adventures. Of slowing my truck to watch a mountain goat drinking water from the side of the road (before he saw me, whirled, and effortlessly picked his way straight up a steep rock incline). Of jet-boating on the Salmon River with a pilot who slowed and lingered long enough for us to watch otters play. Of falling asleep, covered with a sweaty horse blanket, under thousands and thousands of twinkling stars, after an exhausting day of cutting trail. Or best of all, getting different horses or mules to ride every day and learning what made each unique.

How deeply I loved my job on the isolated guest ranch. How surprisingly easy it had become to live without electricity, telephone, television, radio, on-demand hot water, or even a driveway with a mailbox at the end. How fortunate we backcountry folks were to have mail and supplies delivered via airplane. Ray and Carol Arnold of Cascade (as well as the Dorris family in McCall) were greatly appreciated: because of them we had the freedom to live in the middle of nowhere, far from chaos. Someday, I thought, opening my eyes and looking around, even this fiasco of completely losing an orange bag in white snow might turn into a descriptive and funny story.

But tell you what, it wasn't so funny right *then*.

Yet while gazing about at the lodge, the crisscross fencing, my 1890's cabin, the mules, and the outbuildings, I started to feel calmer. From the moment I'd first walked into the ranch, stepping from the shady wagon trail into the enormous meadow, I'd belonged there. Having grown up camping, caving, back-packing, hiking, and riding with a great group of friends, it felt perfectly natural to have ended up living such a pioneer-like lifestyle. But I *did* miss those friends, in addition to my family, and *soooo* wanted to get my hands on their letters…

Then there it came, one of the most beautiful sounds I've ever heard, the hum of a returning airplane. The William Tell Overture (also known as the Lone Ranger theme) automatically started playing in my head. Dashing out to meet it, I leapt like a gazelle over the snow until I made it to the bridge. Topping the mountains, Ray flew right to me, slowing the Cessna as it got lower and lower to the ground. One wing made a brief dip, and I knew he was trying to communicate the location of the bag. Keeping my eyes focused on that spot, I plunged to that area…and found it instantly.

I held the damp canvas firmly with one hand and with the other, waved as hard as I could, over and over, yelling *"thank you thank you thank you thank you!!!"* as he cruised overhead. And even though Ray clearly couldn't have heard me, as the plane gained altitude he tilted one wing yet again, that time to indicate "You're welcome."

*"Ray landed on skis in the winter."*

# CHAPTER 7

# BLIND-SIGHTED

"Shoot it!" Zeke whispered urgently. His lips barely moved. Squatting beside me in the snow, he stared through the scope of his rifle with left eye squinted and right index finger frozen on the trigger. "*Shoot!*"

I hesitated, lowering my .308 Mossberg and looking downhill at the Mule deer buck that was staring up at us curiously. Bedded down under a grove of Ponderosa pines, against the white and green background it looked no bigger than a large brown dot. I was certain I'd miss since my rifle had no scope, but it was worth the try. Especially with Zeke to back me up.

While filling in as camp cook for an outfitter along the Salmon River, I'd been sent up the mountain with Zeke to tear down a drop camp. Together we had swept snow off tents, untied plastic rain covers, and rolled everything tightly into bundles. We'd lowered the support beam and poles and unwound the wires that secured them. All were leaned upright against a grove of trees while axes, shovels, brooms, and wood splitters were carefully hidden in a cache.

A blaze was built in the fire pit and we burned excess hay-baling twine, assorted garbage, and the worn squares of plastic that had covered dirt floors. We emptied the stoves of their ashes and pulled the sooty pipes apart. Before loading the mules with the tents and wooden camp boxes, we sat together on a stump to eat sandwiches and share black coffee from a thermos.

"I haven't seen a single track," Zeke said, swiping his mouth with the back of a sleeve. "The deer may have moved down to the river already." A lifelong hunter, he'd kept a sharp lookout during our steep climb uphill.

"That's okay." I shrugged. "It really doesn't matter if I get one."

"You will," he said confidently.

I grimaced, thinking, 'I doubt it.'

Even though it was great when the hunters were successful, shooting an elk, deer, or bear of my own had never been a goal. My time in Idaho and Montana had mostly been spent cooking, cleaning, picking up guests at the airport, taking them on trail rides, or packing hunters and their gear into campsites. I also hauled game meat to base, loaded it into a pickup and drove it to Grangeville or Lewiston for processing. When only the antlers were wanted, I saved every ounce of meat that could be cut up, wrapped, frozen in a propane freezer, or preserved in canning jars.

Along the way — by asking advice of women who'd spent decades living in the backcountry — I learned how to scrape flesh off hides using a special, curved knife. I learned to add raw bacon when grinding elk or deer hamburger, which added both moisture and flavor. I learned to marinate roasts in red wine and garlic for tenderizing, and to always fry fresh liver with *plenty* of onions and bacon. (It covered the taste. Funny how each man insisted on trying the liver of his own kill, yet rarely ate more than one slice.) And I learned to make lard out of bear fat, a process which took most of a day.

The pieces had to be rinsed free of stray hairs, cut into squares, placed in the largest pot possible, and covered with plenty of water. You boiled and boiled and boiled it over low heat, continually adding more water, until the fat finally cooked down to tiny, curled strips floating in rich, yellow grease. After it had cooled, you strained it through cheesecloth into jars. By morning, the liquid fat would have solidified into a beautifully smooth, white substance that was invaluable to cook with. (Ironically, that same substance doubled as something the crew used to water-proof their boots.) Bear lard was worth its weight in gold to us cooks: substituted half and half with butter, margarine or oleo, it made biscuits, piecrusts, and pancakes so flaky they literally melted in the mouth.

I also (somewhat squeamishly) cooked tongue a few times, guessing at what spices were needed to enhance the flavor. When shaved thin, placed between two slices of bread, and slathered with mayo and mustard, the finished product tasted just like beef. One season, at least a half-dozen hunters ate tongue sandwiches and never even knew it!

It was sobering to realize if one chose to eat meat, something died, so I determined to save everything possible during the butchering process — even the smallest bits of gristle for the dogs. But there *were* limits. I wouldn't cook brains, for instance, or fry up what the boys mischievously referred to as Rocky Mountain Oysters. I didn't have the time or patience to make jerky. (The guys tried it one afternoon, laying raw strips across the grill inside the wood stove over, but didn't tell me. I cranked up the heat to start supper and ended up ruining their experiment.) I also drew the line at bleaching skulls or bones, which removed any remnants of hide, flesh or sinew. It was just too gross; I had good reason.

One particularly horrid afternoon, in need of something to haul rocks with, after wandering from building to building with no luck I'd finally stumbled across a bent metal bucket by the water spigot, between the wood shed and the lodge. Perfect, except that it was filled with green-slimed water and maggots. 'Why do the guys always leave trash laying around?' I thought, kicking at the bucket to empty it.

But as the water ran out, so did a bear skull — fangs first — complete with eerie, shrunken eyes. The crew had left the head to be bleached but again, neglected to give warning. All I remember is running as fast as possible in the opposite direction, waving both hands and screaming hysterically, bringing the boys running from every corner of the property. They brought it up, for fun, every now and then for years because, you know. I had acted like a *girl*.

Zeke couldn't have cared less if I was a woman. In his extended family, both males and females were hardy and highly-skilled outdoors-people. He'd grown up following his parents, two sisters, and grandparents through the woods and was so passionate about scouting, searching for shed antlers, hunting, talking about hunting, planning his hunts, and target-practicing with rifle, bow, crossbow, or muzzleloader it was impossible not to get caught up in the thrill. Maybe it was his attitude, or maybe it was because I never felt judged by him, or maybe I had made my mind up to at least try, but...that's how I ended up hunkered on a steep hillside, high above the Salmon River, with Zeke's busy uncle's unfilled tag in my pocket ("just in case," he'd said encouragingly, patting my shoulder), and snow falling lightly on my shoulders, pointing a rifle downhill at an impossibly distant target.

How on earth Zeke managed to spot that buck in the first place remains a mystery. It was already mid-afternoon when we mounted our horses to head down the mountain, and the shadows were long. Constantly turning in the saddle, he was keeping a careful eye on the string between us, slowing around switchbacks, at rocky sections, and through trees that closely lined the trail, which allowed his mules to ease through without banging their loads. In one smooth motion he'd pulled his gelding up, put a finger to his mouth, and ever-so-silently slid down the off-side of the saddle. He gestured for me to pull my rifle from its scabbard and come to him. Barely breathing, I eased along the line of lightly-blowing mules. "There," Zeke whispered, pointing downward with a slow-moving hand. "See it?"

My first thought was, 'Where?' and the second, 'Are you kidding?' The odds of finding a needle in a haystack were higher; surely, Zeke wasn't serious. Surely, we'd find something much closer if we waited a day or two. Shaking my head, I leaned over to say, "No, I'm not going to try it…"

But the words never came because clearly, Zeke was in a zone. His eyes were burning with the same intensity my own eyes had had in 1973 when I watched Secretariat win the Triple Crown. Or when I saw amazing performances by the Budweiser Clydesdales and the Royal Lipizzaner stallions. In that moment, catching Zeke's intensity, I finally understood that a successful hunt was a rite of passage for certain outdoorsmen and women. Just like I've always shared my love of horses, Zeke sincerely wanted to share with me the thrill of outwitting a deer. For a mere human to take down a wild animal, I'd learned from listening, required the perfect balance of timing, skill, stealth, endurance, shooting ability, patience, weather, and sheer luck. You were pitting yourself against something which had perfect eyesight, hearing, instinct, cunning, and speed on its side — not to mention the ability to completely melt into its surroundings.

Or in my case, you were fortunate enough to stumble across a sleepy buck, bedded down for an afternoon nap, that simply didn't feel the need to move.

"Back me up in case I wound it, okay?" I whispered anxiously to Zeke, and he nodded. His rifle — some gorgeous family heirloom — had already been drawn.

Ever-so-slowly we moved away from the mules down the hillside, crouching behind bare shrubs here and there along the way. The buck continued watching but made no attempt to rise. Coming to a flat spot, Zeke knelt, and I did the same. Taking a deep breath, I thought, 'C'mon girl, you can do this. Just stay calm.'

I lifted the Mossberg and braced the stock against one shoulder, aligning the two, iron sights closest to my nose with the one on the front of the barrel. Snowflakes landed on the dull metal and I paused to flick them off. My arm pit got an itch and I carefully reached under to scratch it. Regardless of heavy wool pants and thermal underwear, one knee started to feel damp, so I cautiously shifted. But Zeke remained motionless.

"Shoot! *Shoot!*" he whispered again, hoarsely that time. Dressed in a tattered, sweat-stained cowboy hat, a flannel shirt, vest, and a neckerchief, he seemed more like a Remington statue than a living, breathing man. But I'd heard some of his bow-hunting tales and knew he could remain frozen for an hour at a time if necessary. Somehow, that topped off my courage. Long, silent seconds went by as I replanted the rifle butt, drew a bead on the deer, held both arms still, and waited for just…the…right…moment. Almost on its own, my right index finger eased against the trigger. Anticipating the kickback, I closed my eyes… and the Mossberg fired.

The blast kicked my shoulder and made both ears ring. Blinking hard and glancing downhill, I noticed a huge puff of snow floating gently to the ground. "You got him!" Zeke yelled, jumping to his feet and taking off running. Nimble as a mountain goat, he rapidly grew smaller and smaller as he dashed down the slope, rifle held out to one side.

For a few moments I knelt there, stunned, before rising to my feet and picking my way down the hillside, sideways. He had leaned his rifle against a tree, leapt behind the buck and grabbed its antlers by the time I got there. His yells turned into shrieks. Flipping the head towards me, then to himself, then back towards me, he hollered, "You got it! You got it! Oh my gosh, *you got it right between the eyes!*"

I barely registered what I was hearing. "What? What did I do?" A trickle of blood oozed down the buck's forehead towards its muzzle. Its wide ears lay limp and blood dripped from them, as well. There was no mistaking it; the bullet hole was dead-center.

"I don't believe this! What a shot! You made a bullseye! *You nailed it right between the eyes!*" Zeke jumped up and for a moment I thought he was going to dip his finger in the bullet hole and swipe blood on my face as part of a ritual. He didn't, so I leaned over to examine my first kill more closely. In guide school, we'd been trained to poke an animal in the eyeball with a long stick (and be prepared to jump back) to make *sure* it was dead, but that clearly wasn't needed here. '*Thank goodness, it never felt a thing*," I thought.

"Wow, this is amazing!" Zeke laid the head down and stood up. He looked at me like I was a Grecian huntress. "How'd you do that?"

"I don't know," I stammered. My eyes were closed."

"Yeah, right!" Zeke laughed; he was so stoked my admission went right over his head. Talking more to himself now, he added, "Oh man, I can't wait to tell the guys...they won't believe this!"

I knelt and touched the deer. It was warm and soft. I stroked its fur gently, marveling at the thickness. Growing up in the hardwood forests of Ohio I'd seen plenty of Whitetails, and even ridden close to some when on Tee, but had certainly never touched one. I almost forgot about Zeke for a moment, admiring that deer, but with the lateness of the hour he got to business.

Sliding a knife from a sheath looped to his belt, he extended it to me handle-first. Silently, I accepted it, weighing it in my hand. When I hesitated, he asked, "Wanna gut it? Ever done that before?"

"Um, no," I admitted. "Never had a chance to."

"I'll show you. Here. Grab the front legs." Zeke took the back ones and we lined the buck out on its side. Lifting the hind leg that was closest to him, Zeke gestured towards the buck's limp and unnervingly exposed private parts. "Start here," he said with authority.

"What?"

"Just pull them straight up and insert the blade in the raised..."

"I'm not touching that!" I interrupted, shocked, stepping backwards. The hunters had never discussed this part of the process when telling their tales, and I didn't recall hearing much about it during training.

"Here, I'll do it." Zeke shouldered me aside, knelt, and swiftly sawed through the hide toward the deer's chest while I watched in fascination. (To this day I've never seen a knife move so fast.) "You don't want to puncture the gut sack," he instructed without turning his head. "If you do, it'll stink to high heaven."

Grunting with effort, with both arms inside the cavity Zeke made a half dozen more cuts at the base of the buck's chest and rolled out the entrails, which were inside a protective bluish membrane. He retrieved a hatchet from the other side of his belt and began rapidly hacking at the joints below each kneecap and hock, twisting sinews and tendons until they sapped apart. As each lower leg broke free, he flung them in the bushes.

When Zeke started to chop off the head, however, I stopped him. I didn't want to leave it behind, taking only the severed antlers. Pride had kicked in and I wanted to show the proof of where the bullet struck. We decided to haul the buck in one piece without cutting it into quarters. While he cleaned his tools and hands in the snow, I hurried up the hill and fetched a pack mule. Cautiously, with the mule's breath blowing behind one ear, I eased my way down, again sideways.

But just as Zeke reached for the lead rope, I grabbed his wrist, near-panicked. "Wait! Wait! We didn't take a picture! I need a picture!" Every successful hunter I'd ever met that year had had one taken with his trophy, in the exact spot where it had fallen.

"I have a camera in my saddle bags." Looking up at the darkening sky, Zeke added hastily, "I'll get it."

There was no time for more than a few poses — snow was coming hard. After tying the deer atop the folded tent and securing the head with hay-baling twine so it wouldn't flop, Zeke and I hustled back up the hill. Bringing up the rear, I grabbed hold of the mule's tail so my climb would be easier. We mounted up and travelled towards camp as safely as we could but still ended up in pitch-darkness, relying entirely on our mounts to find the way.

I couldn't see a hand in front of my face. It was one of the eeriest experiences I've ever had, sitting on a horse with absolutely no concept of when he was about to turn, or how far his front legs and shoulders were going to drop at rocky inclines, or how deep his ankles would get sucked into mud holes. It was like being in a completely unfamiliar room with no light switch, having no idea what furniture was where. I had to trust my mount completely, giving him just enough rein to pick his way (maintaining enough contact to pull his head up if he stumbled, which he thankfully didn't) and riding light in my stirrups, letting knees and the balls of the feet automatically balance the body. "You okay?" Zeke called out every now and then, his voice sounding muffled with three mules between us.

"Great!" I assured him. And I truly was.

The other hunters and guides had already broken into the food boxes and were eating crackers and canned tuna when we pulled up to the hitching rails. The horses and mules that were already tied for the night whinnied welcomes, and at once a tent flap opened and lantern light streamed out. "Is that you, Zeke?" the outfitter called.

"Yup!" Zeke called back.

The outfitter walked towards us, his boots scrunching on the frozen ground. He switched a kerosene lantern from hand to hand while pulling on a black and red checkered coat. The lantern hissed and steamed in the cold air and I caught a whiff of kerosene. "Where the heck you been?"

Zeke jerked his chin towards the mules as he unbridled his horse. "Carolyn shot a deer!"

"She did?"

"Yup, and she made a bullseye!" Zeke looped the bridle around the saddle horn and turned towards his uncle, grinning from ear to ear.

"She *what*?"

"Here, check it out!" Zeke walked over to the buck, proud as if he'd shot it himself, and the outfitter followed, raising the lantern. Flashlights appeared as other men wandered over. They gathered around the buck in a half-circle, some leaning in to get closer looks. It's dull, glazed eyes reflected gray in illumination.

"Well I'll be, our lil' cook there knows how to *shoot*, too?" one of the hunters teased, shining his beam on me.

The others followed suit. "I didn't know Annie Oakley was in this camp!" and "Hey! Rifle Woman!" and "Who knew she had it in her?" they teased.

I wanted to stick around, but my job was in the mess tent. Part of me was scared we were in trouble, but we weren't. Time and time again over supper, Zeke relayed how he'd spotted the buck, how we'd slid off our horses, how we'd eased down the hill and how I'd picked it off with the skill of a sharpshooter. What impressed everyone the most was the fact he had counted off 220 yards while running towards the body. "Heck, I couldn't have made that kind of shot with a scope!" one of the hunters admitted.

And although I made it clear the shot was pure chance, the men graciously behaved like they didn't believe it. One hunter, who was returning home to Louisiana the next morning empty-handed, even took out his wallet and offered me cash for my buck. "Mah wif'," he said in his thick Cajun accent, "iz gonna be mad eef I come home wi' nuh'ting! Af'tuh I spen' all dis money!" I wouldn't have parted with that little rack (which measured a mere 17 inches but was huge to my eyes) for a thousand dollars.

However, long after the dishes had been done, the cook tent cleared, and the blankets pulled back on the cot, I kept seeing that beautiful creature in my head. How pretty his gray-brown hide had been against the pines and snow. How innocent he'd seemed, staring up at us. How strange his body had looked when Zeke and I got to it, so completely still and lifeless.

Like the shock of a branding iron, the enormity of what happened sunk in: *I'd killed something*. On purpose, for no other reason than to prove I could do it, I'd pointed a gun and pulled the trigger. That deer was never coming back. Carrying a firearm was one thing, I understood over that long and sleepless night, but it was a serious, *serious* responsibility. Holding the pillow to my face so the sound wouldn't carry, I burst into tears and sobbed uncontrollably until dawn. That morning, I served the hunters silently, with swollen eyes. Sensing the mood, they cast furtive glances and didn't talk much, either.

Although to this day I'm perfectly willing to help other people cut-up, wrap, freeze, cook, or can their own wild game or beef, I never went hunting again. I share the one-hit-wonder story every now and then, however, since the antlers are on view in the office. But the ending has this addition: sometimes it's best to quit when you're ahead. How could I top that perfect shot, even with my eyes opened?

*"The antlers, plus the photo Zeke took, are on display in the office."*

# CHAPTER 8

# TEAMSTER TRAINING

"Are we still within sight of the lodge?" I asked Karen.

Riding shotgun, she glanced over her right shoulder. "No...I don't see it."

Jim and Shorty, the Belgian draft horses that were pulling our wagon, flicked their ears as I gathered the lines and braced my boots against the foot board. "Hold on then," I told her. "I feel a need for speed!"*

Grinning broadly, she took a grip on the wooden seat as I flipped leather against the backs of both geldings. "C'mon boys. Hup! Hup!" The tug chains jingled louder as they lumbered into trots. Their broad rumps rocked back and forth and their long tails swished. Eight unshod hooves — tossing up large puffs of dust — made muffled clomping sounds along the dirt forest trail.

Karen and I had swayed backwards when the wagon lurched, but as we straightened she exclaimed, "God, this is awesome! I wish we could live here!"

"I wish you could live here, too, Face," I replied, grinning back at her. "You'd be *such* a great hand!"

Karen had shoulder-length blond hair, merry blue eyes and rosy cheeks, but she'd been knick-named "Face" for her wide, toothy smile. Friends since junior high school, we'd frequently gone riding together on her stout Pinto pony, Rascal, and my Tee. Bareback and barefoot, we strolled through quiet neighborhoods, pretending to be mounted policemen on patrol. On dirt stretches we became jockeys, spontaneously bursting into races — which Tee always won, being part Thoroughbred. If the ground was damp from rain, Karen would get plastered with mud from Tee's churning hooves, but it never bothered her. "Good girl, Rascal! We almost caught 'em that time!" she'd laugh after reining up, vigorously slapping the neck of her equally-muddy mount. I can still hear that laughter in my mind from time to time and it is priceless.

After she married Tim (another classmate) and moved to Nashville, we started writing. Somewhere in a trunk I've saved her letters, each written on lined yellow notebook paper and chock-full of pictures and news. When the extra-special one arrived via mail plane, announcing she was coming to visit Idaho, I was beside myself, and from the moment Face arrived it was like we'd never even parted.

Within days she was milking the cow, slopping the hogs and gathering eggs before breakfast. She fed the hound puppies twice a day, chuckling out loud while trying to hold them off long enough to dump milk and kibble into their bowls. She even started Dixie, my two-year-old Quarter horse, by lounging her in the corral.

Karen helped the crew hand-peel bark off Lodge pole pines (each dragged in by the Belgians) for the new cabin they were building. Biting one lip in deep concentration, she mastered the art of rope-braiding. She even tried chewing tobacco. That experiment ended raucous laughter after she gagged and dashed for the outdoor spigot to rinse her mouth.

After breakfast she could be seen strolling across the meadow with Jim and Shorty's giant halters in hand, searching the 500 acres to find them grazing side-by-side. Leading them uphill to the enclosure by the tack room, she tied them at the feed trough and stood on tip-toes to groom each from forehead to fetlocks, softly telling them how handsome they were.

I'll never forget the first time Karen lifted a hoof and exclaimed, "*Geez!* This thing is bigger than a dinner plate!" After securing it between her knees (grunting with great exaggeration), she held one hand out for the pick I was holding. Studying the tiny tool for a moment, she attempted to hand it back to me. "Don't you think a hammer and chisel would do better?" She laughed. Chunks of dirt and rocks hit the ground as she cleaned it, and after finally easing that hoof down Karen straightened, rubbed her back and exclaimed, "Okay, I'm done! No more for me!" But we knew she was having the time of her life.

It was great to have her help with the harnesses, which were too heavy and cumbersome for me to lift by myself. First, Karen and I placed pads and horse collars around Jim and Shorty's necks. Then we lugged the heavy leathers out of the tack room and heaved them onto their broad backs. We snugged the belly bands against their barrels, spread the turnbacks over their spines, and ran the hip drops and breeching across their rears, carefully pulling their tails over the tops.

When it came to bridling, Shorty (who was somewhere in his mid-twenties, the older of the team) had a trick. He raised his head so no one under six feet tall could reach it. I had to climb into the feed trough (crouching so my own noggin didn't whack into the overhang) and ease the snaffle bit to his mouth with the left hand while holding the headstall against his forehead with the right. Usually, one also had to stick a thumb between his droopy lips to open them. "C'mon, big guy, take the bit now… that's a good boy." Sighing deeply, he obliged.

After the bit slid against Shorty's gums I pulled the headstall over his halter and his ears, straightened the cheek pieces, adjusted the blinders, and buckled the throatlatch before jumping down to the ground. Karen did Jim. We separated the long, leather lines, clipped them to the bits and threaded them through terrets along each collar. Finally, I walked around both horses and made sure each clasp, ring, chain and buckle had been completely secured.

The Belgians had been on the ranch for so long they knew the routine — and the three-mile route to the trailhead — better than any handlers. (The road had been closed to motor vehicles by the Forest Service in the 1940's after the area was declared Wilderness.) When I untied each lead rope and looped it around the hames, a quiet alertness came over those gentle giants. They eased away from the feed trough and walked towards the gate as one unit while I followed, holding the lines with the excess draped over one shoulder. We went into the yard, made a wide circle and stopped at the front of the wagon. "Over," I told them and Jim, positioned on the right, carefully side-stepped over the tongue and waited while Shorty lined up to his left. (Sometimes we had to shove on his hip for that last extra inch or two.) Both then stood quietly as Karen raised the tongue, attached it to their collars and hooked Jim's harness chains to the double tree while I hooked Shorty.

If guests were waiting on transportation to the trailhead, the team was driven to the lodge's porch. They stood patiently while luggage, boxes, hunting gear, and people were loaded. From there they swung to the right, walked out the main gate, thudded over the first bridge in the meadow, and sedately paralleled the broodmare pasture on their way towards the forest trail. Separated by crisscross wooden fencing, the mares and foals always trotted, cantered, or bucked alongside but Jim and Shorty stayed steady. Usually, we completed the route, one way, in about an hour.

It was a snail's pace, safe, slow and sure. Unless, of course, there were two lady teamsters in control.

It was the foreman's iron-clad rule that the team never go faster than a walk — but then, he wasn't that great of a driver (and we all knew it). Sometimes, maneuvering through tight twists in the path he scraped trees with the wagon, making the team dance briefly in alarm. He also yanked them in too sharply at the bridges, making their mouths come open. Luckily, he wasn't available on that first morning Karen and I went out alone; he was busy giving fly-fishing lessons. Meantime, the other guys were needed to work on their cabin. The walls and roof had to be finished before hunting season opened, so nobody argued when Karen and I offered to haul hay. (The guys were more than happy to get out of the hot, itchy, back-breaking job. Even the few visitors who had volunteered their services earlier in the week had quickly lost enthusiasm.)

Of all the ranch chores, putting up hay was the most unpleasant. It got down your shirt and your pants. It made you itch and sneeze. Without the protection of long sleeves and gloves, it left red marks on your arms and hands. And it took forever to complete the job since the owner bought 40 tons each summer to feed livestock through the long, brutally cold winters. Hauled from Kamiah in stock trucks, the bales were unloaded in a holding corral at the trailhead and transported through the woods, thirty-three at a time, by a team of Belgians and wagon.

Karen had put up plenty of hay, and she was ready for it. (She not only worked as a horse trainer in Nashville, but her Aunt Carol owned our home town's only boarding, training, and riding stable.) She'd never done it in a wagon, however. We tried not to look too excited as we climbed on the bench seat — me because I was escaping the kitchen and Karen because it was a new experience — and fully aware of the foreman's critical eye, we drove off as sedately as two ladies heading to church. We even waved to the guests who were standing by the creek in their waders, their fly poles dangling as they paused to watch.

But once out of sight we became teenagers again, stealing off in Karen's little blue Volkswagen with Jody, another longtime friend. Karen's permed curls blew gently about her face as the Belgians stepped out eagerly, tossing their heads. The path was straight and smooth, the load was light, and the morning air was cool. I didn't slow the team until we rounded a bend and discovered that a fallen tree blocked our way.

"Whoa, boys," I said, pulling them up. Blowing slightly, they turned their heads from side to side trying to see beyond the blinders.

"Can we drag it, you think?" Karen asked. We climbed down, walked past Jim and Shorty (patting their sides along the way) got good grips and yanked at the trunk. Although slender, it was too heavy to move in one piece. "There's a handsaw under the foot rest," I told Karen as I walked back to the wagon to fetch it.

We took turns with the handsaw (bracing a boot and yanking each time it got stuck), eventually sawing the trunk in half. We shoved both sections off to the side of the path, leaving wood chips dotting the dirt. The geldings, which had been dozing with one hind hoof tipped, straightened lazily as we resumed out places. But that time, after picking up the lines I hesitated. "Want to drive?" I asked my friend, holding them over.

"*Do I!*" Karen's blue eyes widened. "I've been dying to try this since I got here!" She reached out eagerly and took them. Clearly, she'd paid attention because she gathered the excess inches, braced her thumbs against the leather and her feet against the footboard, and leaned slightly forward. "Jim. Shorty. Hup!" she called, and the Belgians obediently stepped out.

"You have to watch Shorty," I instructed, raising my voice over the jangle of tug chains. "He tends to lag behind. Give him a light swish against the rump with the left line and he'll speed up." Sure enough, we hadn't gone twenty yards before Shorty started slowing, testing out the new teamster. Karen flipped the line at him immediately, laughing softly when he hustled to match pace with Jim.

She kept a gentle hold on the geldings' mouths, rocking the leather lines back and forth to keep them steady, until we came to the most challenging section of trail. There were several hairpin turns over a fifty-yard section, and some of the trees had deep notches in the bark where the wagon's sides had struck. I took control again, explaining, "We need to swing the team as wide as possible through a few spots here, just like you'd do with a semi-truck going into an alley." As we approached the first tight turn, I continued, "See that Lodgepole ahead?" She nodded intently. "Aim the team right for it and pull them to the left at the very last moment." Jim and Shorty headed straight towards the pine, and Jim's muzzle just...about...grazed it before I swung both horses hard. "Watch behind us," I added, and Karen's head immediately spun. "See how close the wagon came to the trunks on the left side? You'll have only inches to spare..." She nodded thoughtfully, absorbing the lesson and watching intently as we reined through the next several curves.

At the bridge, I gently pulled Jim and Shorty's chins in before the downward slope, saying, "Easy. Easy. Eeeeeaaaaasy, boys!" They inched along the down side carefully, butts tucked and muzzles nearly touching, and lightly stepped into the muck at the base without splashing. The wagon sank deeply there before popping out with sucking sounds when the horses were given their heads and asked for power. I'd learned the hard way how important it was to ease into those slick, muddy spots. New to the ranch, sitting between the foreman and one of the wranglers and *greatly* looking forward to a shopping trip to Grangeville, I'd gotten splattered from face to red-checked blouse to sandals when the foreman took a bridge too fast. (There were splinters in both hands, too, from clutching the bench seat out of terror.)

Yet riding in the wagon was a blast. I loved driving the team, and I loved how each new group of guests lit up when they climbed in behind me. As for Karen? She *never* stopped grinning. "Face" had on her happy face that day as she learned how to handle Jim and Shorty, and it remained constant throughout those wonderful three weeks we shared together on a ranch in central Idaho.

As we approached the corral I swung the Belgians to the right, then left, making a wide circle before stopping. Without being asked Karen hopped down to open the gate. I backed the geldings until the tail gate had snugged against the hay pile.

"Oh, this is *so awesome!*" she exclaimed as she rolled her shirt sleeves down. "I'm gonna tell Aunt Carol she needs to get a *wagon!*" She pulled her gloves on and scampered to the top of the pile. I waited in the bed as she took a grip on the twines of the first bale and slid it to the edge of the stack. "Heads up, boys!" I called out to the horses a few seconds before she neatly dropped it. The bale hit the floorboards with a *thunk*.

*Thunk...thunk... thunk.* Methodically, Karen lifted, dragged, and tossed the bales while I shoved them side by side and made stair steps, using one knee to help stack. Twice we stopped, wiped sweat off our foreheads, and shared a plastic gallon jug of water. The sun started peeking through the tops of the trees and I looked at it. "That tree we had to cut slowed things down, Face. We'll have to hustle to finish a second load before it gets too hot this morning."

She lowered the jug and nodded. "Okay."

"We'll do two more loads this evening after things cool down."

"What? You mean we get to keep doing this?" She burst into her trademark chuckle.

We placed the final three bales sideways on the top row to anchor the stacks. (I remember thinking with pride that our rows looked even tighter than the ones the guys made.) I moved the team forward so Karen could close the gate to keep the elk, deer, moose, and cattle out and we drove home slowly with the axels of the wagon creaking and our backs resting against shifting, rustling hay.

Nobody was in the creek fly-fishing, but upon hearing our approach one of the guys jumped down from the unfinished cabin's rafters, ran across the yard and swung the double gates open. Although Jim and Shorty had walked the whole way back, I urged them to fast trots right after we crossed the meadow's shorter bridge so they could get the running start needed to clear the steep incline towards the barn. (It was the only section where the foreman allowed speed.) The muscles in their powerful hindquarters churned as Jim and Shorty leaned into their collars, extended their necks and with hooves pounding, dust flying, and chains rattling, towed close to 2500 pounds of hay, wagon, and women uphill. "Oh, cool!" Karen burst out at my side. Their necks were covered with sweat and their nostrils were red, wide, and blowing when we stopped by the barn, but their eyes were alert and their ears were twitching. They'd had a good time, too.

Karen and I unhooked the lines, removed the bridles, hung them over the hames, detached the horses from the wagon, and led them into the corral to rest under the shade of the overhang. We unloaded the bales and stacked them neatly by the generator-powered hay ladder. By the time we'd finished, Jim and Shorty had cooled off enough to have water, so we lead them to the creek for long drinks. Both had caught second winds and were raring to go when we headed off for the second load. Once we were out of sight of the lodge, I handed the lines over to Karen. She urged the pair into trots and we swayed back and forth to their rhythm.

For the rest of those trips it was Karen who swung the Belgians through the tight spots along the forest path and reined them in at bridges. It was Karen who waited while I jumped down and opened the gate at the hay corral so she could back the wagon in. And it was Karen who carefully guided the team and their heavy load towards home, handing over the lines only as we came within sight of the lodge.

Mark, who was a decent cook, volunteered to fix supper that evening so we could make the last drive, returning right at dusk. I'll never, ever forget how Face and I worked together just like that team, loading, stacking, unloading and re-stacking a total of 132 bales which ranged from 60 to 80 pounds apiece. We even thoroughly groomed Jim and Shorty, combed their manes and tails, picked their hooves, and wiped down the harnesses before quitting for the night. Our arms hurt, our backs and shoulders ached, and our hands were sore but when we sat down to grilled hamburgers, potato chips, and pork and beans we ate like the teamsters (and speedsters) we were. The guys were impressed, especially since we never asked for help, but the foreman was suspicious. "You girls made pretty good time today," he pointed out sarcastically.

"We didn't mess around," I replied without batting an eye.

"Did you run them?"

"Are they lathered?"

He backed off.

And I'll never forget the stunned looks on everyone's faces when — as the following day's schedule was being discussed under the glow of a single propane light — Karen suggested sweetly, "If one of you will cook breakfast *and* dinner for the rest of the week, Carolyn and I will keep on haying."

*"Jim and Shorty wait to haul a load of gear from the airstrip to the lodge."*

*This came from a popular movie of the time called "Top Gun." Karen got it; we'd seen it together.

# CHAPTER 9

---

# CAT FISHIN'

Standing on the edge of the porch, I cupped both hands to my mouth and hollered, "Time's up!" Just to be sure the crew heard me, I vigorously rang the cast-iron triangle that hung from a nail off a beam.

Reluctantly, four crew members lifted poles from the stream that flowed through the meadow. They wound up their lines, gathered their stringers and tackle boxes, and lifting their knees high in the tall grass that grew by the water, headed for the bridge. Accusations, teasing, and laughter drifted up to the lodge. A few of them shoved at each other.

Scattered about on wooden chairs and benches, the summer trip guests sipped their coffees. It was barely eight o'clock. "Looks like they caught a bunch," one murmured. He leaned forward and tapped my shoulder, asking, "Are you going to fry those trout up for breakfast?"

"You bet!" I replied.

The boys hadn't gone fishing to feed everyone, however. For an hour Pat, Travis, Mark and Eddy had been engaging in a knock-down, drag-out battle and the stakes were very high: whoever won got out of catching horses for the next two weeks.

Free time was premium when you worked on a guest ranch, and sleep was our most precious commodity. A fishing competition winner not only earned that extra hour each morning but all that went with it: he didn't have to dress by flashlight; walk uphill to the tack shed for halters and buckets of grain; and traipse around a 500-acre meadow in search of free-range horses — all before a cup of coffee. (It was worse during hunting season when the weather was bad.)

One summer morning, I held off breakfast as long as possible while we waited on Travis. "He left when it was barely light out," I heard Mark say to Pat through the open window of the porch, where they were sitting side by side.

"Eh, he probably circled around and went back to bed," Pat responded.

Guests and crew finally gathered around the dining room picnic table to eat eggs that were rubbery, pancakes that were chewy and sausage that was dry. It was then Travis finally showed up at the back door. His face was nearly as red as his hair, which was plastered to his head when he took off his hat. "Where you been, dummy?" Eddy asked. "We should have been saddled and gone an hour ago!"

"Those *^{>^*< horses!" Travis thundered as he surged toward the table. "I just made two laps around that entire meadow, trying to find them!"

"So where were they?"

He threw his arms out in frustration before flopping down on the bench seat in a huff. "They were up by the corral the entire time! All I had to do was open the gate and the ^"_*#^ walked right in!" He glanced at the guests and mumbled, "'Scuse my French" before pointing an accusing finger at Mark. "It was your turn to catch this morning. You know it."

"Not my fault if you can't keep track." Mark shrugged and raised his eyebrows wickedly. "I heard you shut off that obnoxious wind-up alarm and when you reached for your pants, I decided you could have at 'er." Travis flipped him a quick, finger-related gesture, but you could tell it was in fun. The guys often argued over whose turn it was to wrangle. In fact, they argued a great deal of the time, however good-naturedly.

During guide school, two of the students stumbled across a lone can of beer in a stream and you'd have thought they'd found a fist-sized chuck of gold. No telling how long it had been in there — we figured it had washed downstream from some distant campsite — but when they saw it wedged between rocks they both lunged so fast they nearly knocked each other into the water.

Base camp rang with shouts (mostly obscenities and assorted references to each other's mothers) as they grappled, each with one hand on the can. Around and around they went in a mutual head lock. One lost his ball cap and the other, his sunglasses. Finally, our trainer pulled out a deck of cards and suggested a game of Twenty-One with the winner getting the beer. Three forehead-mopping, face-scrunching rounds followed while the rest of us hovered around the picnic table. (It was good they decided to do best of three. It gave the beer's foam bubbles a chance to settle.)

The winner leapt back from the bench seat, jumping and pumping both fists in the air — understandable since none of us had tasted alcohol in forever. We'd also been working hard in the hot sun, so we watched enviously as he wiped off the lid with the tail of his T-shirt, popped the tab and lifted the can to his lips. "Ahhhhhh," he announced (inhaling deeply and closing his eyes for effect). "Best beer I've *ever* had."

The loser scowled up at him. "I saw it first," he griped. "At least you could share."

"Okay," the winner said cheerfully. He bent his head back and drained all but a dribble. "Here." He set the can on the table, spun it a few times so we could hear the few remaining tablespoons of liquid sloshing about, and added (with eyes wide and innocent), "I don't have hoof and mouth disease or anything like that. At least, not last time I checked…"

Like lightening, the loser sprang from his seat and went for him, attempting another wrestling move. Both ran full tilt through the forest, weaving in-between the trees and squealing like little girls.

I witnessed men coming from different directions, strolling towards the outhouse, and suddenly bursting into foot races to see who could reach the doorway first. I caught them drinking directly out of the one-gallon milk jar, passing it back and forth while noisily accusing each other of leaving backwash. And I absolutely loved their most popular prank — using up the warm water in the round, plastic, outdoor solar shower and then discreetly refilling it with ice water from the creek, hooking it back up for a buddy, and innocently claiming "There's plenty of warm left, I didn't use much." But while on the ranch, it was the fishing derbies that brought out the best of the jokes, ribbing, and competitive spirits.

As the crew came closer to the lodge, the remainder of the guests drifted down from their rooms, some still dressed in robes. The foreman came down from the corral. I went into the kitchen, moved skillets from the wood stove's surface to the warming oven, and stepped back outside. Lester, who was just a four-month-old kitten at the time, peeked up from the sides of the floor boards. His Siamese-blue eyes were crossed. "Oh, come here, you pretty baby," one of the women cooed, leaning over and scooping him onto her lap.

The crew clomped onto the lower deck, laying their gear to one side. "Travis kept his fly in the water for at least ten seconds after you rang the bell," Pat tattled.

"Did not!" Travis sputtered.

"Mark snuck up behind Pat and slipped a trout off his stringer. He was hidden by the huckleberry bushes, but I know it was him," Eddy added.

"Are you crazy?" Mark shoved him.

"Cheater!" Eddy countered.

The four continued to badger each other as they retrieved their fish and carefully laid each out, nose to tail fin, on the rough-cut wooden boards. Intrigued, Lester slithered off the guest's knees and headed straight for the line-up. "Hey, get the cat out of here!" Eddy shouted.

"Yeah, he might snatch one," Pat agreed.

"Are you kidding? Those trout are bigger than he is!" one of the onlookers observed, snickering. Just to be safe, I lifted Lester by the belly and dumped him over the side of the porch.

The cutthroat and rainbow trout were only between six and eight inches long and the boys had caught their limits. Pat and Eddy were eliminated right away since their fish-lines were shortest. But Mark and Travis had lines that were nearly neck and neck. The competition was so close that every quarter-inch made a difference. Bent at the waist, both jockeyed for extra length by carefully straightening each fish body... easing a nose off a tail fin until it barely touched...realigning any fish that had feebly flopped out of place...or flattening a tail that had started to curl. When the boys accidentally bumped heads, there was another brief scuffle.

The foreman leaned in closer for a final inspection. Some of the guests stood up for better views. Murmurs of excitement grew when it became apparent the winning line was going to make it by mere scales. But then...

Like a shot Lester darted between the clusters of legs, grabbed one of the fish behind its gills and staggered off, growling, with his chin held high and a tail fin dragging between his back legs. Stunned, no one moved to stop him. We never had time; he disappeared beneath the porch as quickly as he'd come.

You could have heard a pin drop. We stared down at the remaining fish, at each other, and at Mark and Travis, whose jaws were hanging open in dismay. Someone quipped, "Game over!" and we all started laughing. It went on and on until the guests were wiping tears.

As the noise died down, Travis wiped his hands on his blue jeans. "Mark," he said, sternly addressing his co-worker, "I demand a rematch... after we've killed that cat."

*"Trout were plentiful in the stream by the lodge and at high mountain lakes."*

# CHAPTER 10

# OUT OF THE HOUSE

(A version of this appeared in the October 2017 issue of *IDAHO* Magazine.)

The ranch guest—I think her name was Millicent—stared at me open-mouthed. Her jaw grazed the elegant silk scarf draped around her neck. "The what?" she asked, wrinkling her nose.

"The outhouse," I repeated. "We're in the middle of a drought. It will help if everyone uses it. At least during the day," I added hastily as her expression grew increasingly sour.

Millicent, who'd flown to Idaho from Boston a few days earlier, made a snorting sound. Tall and stately, with Dutch-boy gray hair and a square jaw, she was formidable. "I don't think so," she replied firmly, squaring her shoulders.

I sighed. Millicent was on a week-long trip with two other couples (the husbands were surgeons) and it was shaping to be a long one. Although everyone but Millicent was having a ball vacationing in the middle of nowhere (one couple even insisted on sleeping on the porch, under the stars) there had been issues. One was her insistence that their personal cocktail hour be held from 5:00 to 6:00 each evening, regardless of when dinner was ready. Another was her habit of letting the water run while brushing her teeth. Then there was the reluctance to use the outhouse. Weary of her lack of understanding, I asked bluntly, "Would you prefer the tank to run dry right in the middle of a shower or a flush? Because no doubt that's what's gonna happen."

She opened and closed her mouth a few times during the stare-down the followed. Unable to come up with a response, she spun and went searching for her husband.

The lodge had just one bathroom, which came complete with a shower, tub, sink, and modern commode. Two globe-covered propane lamps, lit by matches, provided light on either side of the mirror. It was surprisingly modern and comfortable, provided you didn't mind the twenty-minute wait for water to heat, or keeping your bathing time short so other people got turns.

Whoever had designed the system did a wonderful job. (Except he didn't bury the pipes quite deep enough and one sub-zero night, they froze and didn't thaw for four months. That was a looooong winter.) Water came from an underground spring and was captured in a ten-by-ten-foot wooden box lined with plastic. It flowed downhill through two pipes that supplied the shower, tub, toilet, kitchen sink, and a slender, metal, cylinder-shaped holding tank located behind the cook stove. To heat water in the holding tank, you squeezed between the stove and a wood bin, knelt, stuffed paper and small chunks of wood into a tiny firebox, and lit things. While puttering about in the kitchen I constantly monitored the tank, adding more wood as needed. You could tell when the water was hot simply by running a hand up and down the cylinder.

"Shower's ready!" I'd holler.

If we were in hunting season, filthy men in bathrobes and slippers — carrying toothbrushes, toothpaste and razors — literally slid across the waxed floor and lunged towards the bathroom door. In the summer, though, when families were in for fly-fishing, hiking, or horseback riding, the rule was "ladies first."

During poor Millicent's vacation, we were experiencing the worst of a years-long water shortage. It had gotten so severe the holding tank's flow had been reduced to a mere trickle. By August, all guests were being encouraged to not only use the outhouse but the outdoor shower, too. Every day, with one five-gallon bucket in each hand, crew members trudged back and forth, back and forth, to the creek in the meadow to scoop water from the deepest spot, scale the hill, and dump it into a fifty-gallon barrel. Set over a fire pit, the barrel was encircled by large rocks plus a screen that prevented sparks from flying. Again, you had to wait for the water to heat but it was worth it.

Through a garden hose, the warmed water gravity-flowed to a

showerhead that was secured with duct tape in a three-sided wooden stall (which had a wooden floor so your feet wouldn't get muddy). You could shampoo your hair, enjoy the mountain view, and watch horses, elk or deer grazing in the meadow all at the same time. An advantage to showering outdoors was we could linger since the barrel held four or five times more water than the kitchen's cylinder tank.

For the most part, guests didn't mind "roughing it"; they chalked up outdoor plumbing as a true, primitive, isolated, non-electric ranch experience. In shorts or sundresses, holding towels and wash cloths, they cheerfully sat in the sunshine and waited their turns. They visited with each other, read books, played with the ranch cats and hound puppies, watched the chickens pecking about, or of course, walked across the yard to the outhouse when necessary.

Regardless of Millicent's deep disdain of it, the outhouse on that guest ranch was deluxe. Built high off the ground to allow for the deepest possible holes, it boasted three wide steps, a shingled roof, and barn wood siding. The double-dutch doors had latches for privacy, and inside were three smooth seats with lids, two for adults and a shorter version for children.

Although I certainly never went inside the outhouse with a companion, other did — in particular, sisters, daughters and mothers, who were exceptionally close. "Want to come with me?" they'd ask each other after dismounting from a trail ride or getting up from the dinner table.

"Sure!" Off they'd go across the dried-up grass.

Only one guest ever objected more strongly than Millicent, and that was one of my brother's two small daughters. Shortly after his family had flown in I heard her yelling clear down to the kitchen. Barely four at the time, she was standing by the smaller seat, red-faced with her eyes squeezed shut, squalling, "I'm not sitting on that!" when I hurried up. Still wearing an apron and rubber gloves, fearful she'd been bitten by a spider, I peered over the lower Dutch door. My niece looked up and glared.

Her mother was trying to reason with her. "It won't hurt you, darling. It's just an outdoor potty. Lots of people use them…"

"Noooo! I won't sit on that hole! It's dark!"

"There's nothing down there, I promise! Really, it's fun to use an outhouse. Aunt Carolyn does it all the time...don't you?" She glanced up at me beseechingly.

I nodded very seriously, choking back laughter. "Yes! Yes! I do! It's great," I hastened to assure my niece. "Here, let me come in." Bluffing, I reached inside to unhook the latch.

"Noooooo," my niece wailed. *"I'm not sitting on that hole! Noooooooooooooooooooooooo!"* With her lower lip out, the little girl scowled vehemently at us. Both chubby hands retained a death grip on her flowered pants.

We ended up hauling water so she could use the commode in the lodge.

To make the outhouse experience as pleasant (and sanitary) for visitors as possible, I scrubbed it once a week with a broom and hot, soapy water, being careful to knock down webs and hornet nests. Extra toilet paper was enclosed in coffee cans, pictures were tacked onto walls, and plastic flowers were either artfully displayed in vases or shoved between cracks in the logs. For night-lights, two candles (in mason jars) and a matchbox were tucked high on a shelf.

Eventually someone built a magazine rack in one corner. The reading material varied depending on what guests left behind, but we made do with outdated newspapers, hunting and sports magazines, gossip weeklies, and crossword puzzle paperbacks. We even got lucky with a high-dollar travel publication, although I never got to read it. The crew immediately nabbed that one for their cabin. They tore out a particularly lifelike picture taken by an underwater photographer of a piranha heading straight for the camera. Up close against a solid black background, the creamy scales, beady eyes and razor-blade teeth looked especially menacing — at least to me since I'm the one who got punked* by it.

Right before bedtime, I'd turned on a flashlight and walked from my cabin, past the storage shed, to the outhouse. Soft lantern and propane lights were coming from the bunkhouse and the lodge but I saw no human forms or shadows. Following protocol, however, I knocked on the side of the little building before entering. "Anybody in there?" No answer.

I went up the steps, closed both doors, put one end of the flashlight in my mouth, lifted the nearest lid . . . and then jumped back and squealed. My flashlight hit the floor and broke. In the pitch darkness, batteries went rolling in all directions. The guys, hearing the scream (and accompanying curse) through their open windows, immediately burst into laughter, "It's Carolyn! You got Carolyn!"

One of the rascals had used cellophane to attach the piranha picture to the ring of the seat, making it appear to be coming straight out of the darkness below. With shaking hands I patted around for the candles and lit one. "Very funny, you guys, very funny!" I shouted back, which only made them laugh harder. But after my wits returned I started giggling. It really was a clever prank.

During daylight hours, with both doors open, the view from the outhouse was beautiful. It took in a corner of the broodmare pasture, a section of the creek, and a grove of quaking aspens. Under normal amounts of rain and snow, clover grass grew thick and richly green. Several of the ranch's mares, in addition to Rosie the milk cow, gave birth in that pasture each year. The foals and the calf entertained us as they nursed, napped in the sun, explored, or chased each other nose-to-tail, nipping at each other's hocks.

But you could watch them from the porch, as well. No need to sit and...stay.

To be frank, with an outhouse the secret is to take a deep breath, hold it for as long as possible, and enjoy for the sake of nostalgia. I recall how one thirteen-year-old girl from Indianapolis truly adored the simple yet functional building because it reminded her of the "Little House on the Prairie" books she'd grown up on. Unlike most other guests, she tended to linger, taking her time behind closed and latched doors (probably, in part, to escape two pesky brothers). One afternoon, however, she was rudely interrupted.

Right as she was reaching for a gossip magazine she heard, "Git outta there! C'mon, hurry up! Git!" in a deep and highly irritated male baritone voice.

The teen hesitated, surprised that someone would speak so forcefully. "I'll be just a minute," she called out hesitantly.

"I said git outta there! Git! Git!"

Thinking someone was having a digestive emergency the girl made a hasty exit, slipping around the side while looking over her shoulder. As it turned out, the yelling had come from a new wrangler at the corral fifteen paces away. He was urging dawdling mules through the opened gate.

"I didn't know *what* to think," she relayed to us at the table that night. "I thought he really, *really* had to go."

*"As outhouses go, the one on the ranch was a beauty."*

*Credit for this perfect word goes to the person who created the TV show, "Punked," also known for great gags.

# CHAPTER 11

---

# MAGGIE-MADE

Plates, glasses, cups, napkins, and silverware for thirteen people had been set on the dining room table. The Lazy Susan in the center was crowded with home-churned butter, salt, pepper, cranberry sauce, and stuffing. It was flanked by two towel-covered baskets, one filled with yeast rolls and another, cornbread.

At eye-level, in the wood stove's warming oven, sat a gooey pan of yams smothered in brown sugar, marshmallows and cinnamon, a large bowl of bacon-drenched green beans, and another with potatoes that had been mashed with garlic cloves and chives. On the lid covering the water reservoir were two fragrant pecan pies. And on top of the stove sat the crowning glory: a twenty-two-pound turkey, its skin glowing golden brown after half a day in the oven. The kitchen smelled heavenly.

Once again "Maggie," a beautiful, cast-iron and nickel-plated, turn-of-the-century Monarch, had helped prepare a most wonderful meal. Swiping sweat off my neck with one hand while stirring with the other, I smiled as the finishing touch, gravy, began to thicken.

Although there were several feet of snow outside and icicles hung from the roof, it was warm and toasty inside the lodge. Recreational snowmobiling season was winding down that first week in March but I had one last large, hungry group to feed. Centrally located within 200 miles of groomed Forest Service trail, the guest ranch was a well-known stopping point for snowmobilers. Some wanted coffee and snacks. Others needed to unthaw. This group, however, had come all the way from Seattle,

Washington, rented hotel rooms and snow machines in Grangeville, Idaho, and booked a day trip…but they'd left all their manners behind.

As scattered as a vanload of two-year-olds, they'd opened every single gate on the grounds, barged into my personal cabin, ignored the lodge's sign requesting they "Please remove all boots and snowsuits on the porch", tracked snow and mud upstairs while checking out the sleeping quarters, and formed a long, impatient line to the single bathroom, meeting my suggestion to use the outhouse with blank and somewhat hostile stares. Of course, my patience had been worn thin by that time of year — snowmobilers often stopped in randomly (nothing like being in a rocking chair, with a book, by the heat stove, and glancing out the window to see headlights rapidly approaching) — but although I took those surprises in stride, *this* group truly vexed me.

No matter the time of year, visitors to the ranch tended to be enthralled by the sensation of stepping back in time. They quickly adjusted to being without television or radio. They rummaged around in the trunk that held board games, pulled out favorites, and gathered around card tables for competitions. They clapped and sang along when we played live music on guitar, mandolin, fiddle, or piano. They sat around the table after supper sharing stories: *everyone* has a story. And many wanted to try their hands at milking Rosie, saddling horses, carrying wood for the stove, or holding and petting the hens. But this group was fixated on much different, more modern things. They didn't even care to build a snowman.

Picking up on the idle talk that floated to the kitchen from the living room, I learned that one man was anxious to return to a landline to check the progress of his stock. Another was annoyed by the absence of bourbon in his fresh-made eggnog. Still another longed to be watching his favorite sports show. As for the women, they were dismayed to discover the propane fixtures in the bathroom weren't satisfactorily bright enough to reset runny mascara or reapply eyeshadow. (Goggles do a number on you.) "Where's the light switch in here?" the first occupant had complained, poking her head around the door.

"We don't have electricity," I reminded her, muttering to myself, "did you bother to read the brochure?"

"Are you serious? I can't see a thing in the mirror!"

"You look fine, Cynthia," a friend assured her from the piano bench, absently patting her own over-sprayed hair (which had been mussed by a helmet).

Aside from requests for towels, hangars, Kleenex and a blow-dryer (loved that one), I was completely ignored. That was hard since I was accustomed to having people pull up seats on the barstools by the kitchen counter and engage in pleasant conversation. My feelings grew increasingly sour, especially after one woman scoffed "that girl can't hear us" when another raised her voice to ask about the ranch's history. By the time their food was ready, I was anticipating how sweet it was going to be to hear those snowmobiles fire up and watch their tail lights grow small in the distance.

Satisfied the elaborate dinner had come together flawlessly, I reached for an antique gravy boat, inserted a ladle, and set it on the table with a flourish, announcing, "Suppertime!" Although it took a while to get everyone settled (it's awkward to lift legs over bench seats when one is wearing knee-high, Vibram-soled boots, and snowsuits that have been unzipped halfway down and left to hang from the waist), soon there were the pleasant sounds of utensils clinking against plates. Efficiently, I retrieved near-empty bowls and platters and refilled them. I wiped up spills with clean, pretty, dish towels. I poured coffee. I fetched more milk, cream, and cottage cheese from the snowbank outside the kitchen window. And when I heard Maggie's crackles slowing down, I leaned 'way over the wood box — it was practically empty by that point — to gather more fuel.

As I straightened with an armload, the same woman who'd assumed I was deaf spoke up again, gesturing towards the kitchen. "Isn't it nice how they're able to manufacture electric stoves these days to look vintage?" she remarked. Daintily reaching for a second roll with fake pink fingernails, she added, "It provides such a *rustic* feel…don't you think?"

Her back had been towards me that afternoon as she sat in the living room, so she hadn't seen any food preparations, but still, I was startled. Not knowing what to say, I froze and stared.

Maggie taught by the sink-or-swim method. It was simple: guests and crew had to be fed so I had no choice but improve my skills quickly. What helped was she was so intriguing, it made cooking fun. In fact, I grew to love it so much that I gave her a name.

Cookstoves talk. Even when making beds upstairs I could tell when she needed stoking by the assorted tings, pops, and snaps she made and how loud, soft, fast, or slow they were. (On average, more fuel was needed every 45 to 60 minutes. We didn't have many hardwoods in the mountains, and pine burns fast.) I learned where the hottest burners were (directly over the firebox) by moving pans of water around and gauging how long it took them to boil. I figured the easiest method to estimate oven temperature (the built-in thermometer was broken) was to stick an arm inside. And I learned the hard way you had to rotate breads, roasts, cakes and casseroles every ten to fifteen minutes — otherwise, whatever side was closest to the wood box might either brown too fast or burn.

Since woodstoves aren't self-cleaning (discovered after ash overflowed the metal catch box below the grate), every few weeks I let the fire die down completely, opened a trap door at Maggie's base, plopped onto the floor and used a special tool to scrape out the soot and sticky tar that had gobbed up inside her. I scrubbed her surfaces with steel wool to loosen what had spilled over and hardened and I polished the ornately-scrolled, nickel-plated features with an old toothbrush to make her shine. Maggie *had* to look good. She wasn't just the most important tool in the kitchen; she was the centerpiece of the entire building.

It was surprising to discover that once Maggie got warmed up, cooking on her was much easier than on conventional stoves. The six burners, as well as the main oven and the warming oven, were always on. All I had to do was shift pots, pans, or skillets around to the appropriate areas. The only, minor inconvenience was you had to stay close to the lodge for some projects. Luckily, there were plenty of other chores to do while I lingered.

In-between stirring, basting, or rotating food, I sometimes worked at the treadle sewing machine in one corner of the living room. It had been a mere decoration before my Engineer father oiled it and fashioned a leather belt to run the wheels. (My mother showed me how to thread the bullet-shaped bobbin.) I started out repairing sheets and pillowcases, but after a year or two got good enough to make a flannel robe — always needed in the backcountry.

To make it work you placed your foot on the large pedal by the floor, gave the wheel on the right a strong turn with your right hand, and then kept up a steady, rolling motion to keep the needle going. Of course, my knee banged against the bottom of the wooden desk that housed the ancient machine — it was made for much smaller women — but I liked the soft clackity clackity clackity sound it made and the smooth, tight stitches that formed as fabric was pushed gently underneath the needle.

I also practiced the piano, sometimes two to three hours every day, while keeping an eye on the stove. It was good to stay in practice; people like to hear it played. I swept the floor, polished windows, ground extra coffee beans, dusted, put game pieces away, straightened sleeping areas, or worked on grocery or camp supply lists. Sometimes, after going to my own cabin for awhile, I'd momentarily forget about Maggie. But always, an alarm bell went off in the back of my head and I'd dash across the yard to find just…enough…glowing coals left to fire her up again.

Some mornings, Maggie was fired up quietly, in the semi-darkness — like the time we had six hunters from New York who were exhausted from airport delays on top of a three-hour time difference. Not wishing to wake them prematurely, I lit a candle and slipped into the pantry to muffle the noise of crumpling newspapers. Creeping back out to the kitchen, I set the wadded papers in the grate, placed slivers of wood on top, and touched the candle to one end. Slowly, things smoked, curled, turned orange and caught fire.

All three vents had been opened to add air, and I watched as flames shot up the smoke stack. Pushing an aluminum coffee pot — which had been loaded the night before — over the hottest burner, I eased onto a bench to wait for it to perk. (No point in starting breakfast until after caffeine; was 3:15 am and I was in a coma.) Suddenly there was a thumping sound upstairs. Even though I'd closed the door to the sleeping area, one of the hunters had risen. 'Oh no….' I remember thinking. Sure enough, down the stairs he came dressed in a blue and white striped robe and leather slippers. He mumbled "morning" before closing the door to the bathroom. A second later he stepped back out. "Would you please show me where to turn the light on?"

"Of course!" Shielding the candle so it wouldn't go out, I carried it across the floor, entered the bathroom, held the flame to the cloth-like mantle inside a wall-mounted globe, and turned the fixture's handle down to release propane. There was a brief hissing sound before the mantle puffed to life, emitting a soft yellow light from its center. "Thanks," the hunter said, rubbing his eyes.

I returned to the kitchen and touched the side of the coffee pot. It was barely warm. The New Yorker, his hair slicked down by water, shuffled from the bathroom to the kitchen and paused to lift a cup from a stack at the end of the counter. "The coffee's not ready yet," I told him but like a sleepwalker, he lifted the pot from the stove and started pouring.

By the light of the candle, which had now been placed atop Maggie, he squinted. "Hey, this is just water," he exclaimed.

"I know. It hasn't perked."

"When will it be ready?"

"Maybe 15 or 20 minutes....?"

"You're kidding." He set the pot down and turned.

I shrugged. "You may as well settle in. Wood stoves take awhile."

He glanced around. "Don't you have a microwave?"

I gestured first towards the candle and then towards the bathroom, where propane light poured dimly through the open door. "Remember? We don't have electricity. Give it a few days, you'll get used to it."

Sighing, he set the cup down, walked around the table, and lowered himself across from me. Neither of us spoke for a few minutes. He finally asked, "Can I have the newspaper?"

"Um...sorry, we don't get one out here."

"Wow. No coffee *and* no paper." He leaned back against the wall. "The guys weren't kidding when they said this place was primitive."

"Great, isn't it?" I responded cheerfully. He snorted, folded both arms across his chest and closed his eyes.

A few minutes later there was more movement upstairs and another man joined our party. "Mornin'!" he said with animation. "Coffee ready?"

"No," we answered in unison. I added, "It hasn't perked yet."

"We're waiting on the wood stove," the first guy informed him.

The second guy, Bill (I remembered his name from checking him in) stopped in mid-reach for a cup. "Seriously?" He looked puzzled. "Isn't there an electric burner for back-up?"

"Bill, *there's no electricity here.* You picked this trip, remember?"

"Right. Right. I did." Bill sat too, staring at Maggie hopefully as if he would make her go faster. Hearing more footsteps upstairs, I circled the kitchen and living room and lit all the propane lights. One by one the other New Yorkers gathered around the table, making small talks and holding cups.

Eventually, they got their coffee and proclaimed it was well worth the wait. All of them said that made on a wood stove, with generous dollops of thick, fresh cow's cream, it was the best they'd ever tasted. *Everything* tasted richer and better when made on Maggie's smooth, black, cast iron surface. I don't know exactly what it was, but she just added something special.

Senior ranch guests remembered their mothers or grandmothers cooking on woodstoves. Younger people who had never seen one leaned in curiously to find out how Maggie worked. (Some tried their hands with her, too, but gave up quickly. A body gets sweaty, fast, when standing close to that much heat.) No one from the Seattle group, however, even acknowledged her.

Now, as I stood by the wood box, with damp hair pushed back from my forehead and burn marks on one arm from bumping the top of Maggie's red-hot grate, I stared at the woman with pink fingernails and wondered if she had enough sense to place the word "wood" together with "stove." She didn't. "Randolph...we should get one for the summer home."

"Hmmmm? Sure..." her husband responded without looking up from the turkey platter he was spearing.

She pointed towards Maggie with a fork. "An old-fashioned-looking electric stove like that would go great in there."

"Yes, dear. Certainly. Pass the yams, please, Walter..."

"It's so quaint..." She turned her head to the side, studying.

"It's a *wood* stove," I interrupted, nodding down at my armload of fuel.

The woman shook her head. "No, it isn't," she said firmly.

"Yes, it is. There's no electricity on this ranch."

"Well, it's propane then," she countered.

"I should know, I work here. It's a *wood* stove."

"It couldn't be!" She straightened her shoulders. "How did you make all this?" Gesturing across the food-laden table, she added, "That's not possible."

*What*? Not possible? On *Maggie*? Together we'd canned hundreds and hundreds of jars of applesauce, game meat, salsa, jams, jellies, and even milk. (The boys used to bring me raspberries, blackberries, and chokecherries in the summer when they took days off to fish the Salmon River. One August, trying to keep the heat high enough for the jams to boil, it got so unbearable that after peering through each lodge window to make sure staff and guests were gone, I discreetly removed my shirt.) Daily, we'd created fresh breads, rolls, muffins or cinnamon buns. We'd fried eggs, turned bacon, boiled potatoes...the list was endless. Making three large meals a day for anywhere from six to 23 people, we'd worked as a perfectly synchronized team. And each and every time I fired that elegant, perfectly functioning, grand old lady up, I silently marveled over her usefulness, her beauty, and her practical design.

Abruptly, I tucked the wood under my right arm, reached for a pot holder with the left and opened the door to the grate. Stuffing the wood inside, I snapped open all three vents. There was a flaring sound and the wood started popping like popcorn. Snatching a lid lifting tool, I flipped one of the heavy, round stove eyes off: it banged against Maggie's hard surface. Bolstered by the sudden input of air, red and yellow flames shot eight to 10 inches upwards from the open hole. I stood with one hand on my hip and pointed with the tool. "See?" I challenged the woman. "*This is a wood stove. Seeeeeeeeee?*"

Wide-eyed, she stared at me with her mouth in an O. Her companions looked alternately confused, interested, embarrassed, or amused. A few discreetly elbowed each other. Randolph didn't skip a beat, though. "I'll get you a *wood* stove then, Patricia," he said smoothly, "if you promise you'll learn how to cook on it like *she* does."

*"Maggie had six burners, a warming tray, a regular oven and a hot water reservoir."*

# CHAPTER 12

# APRON STRINGS

Colorado, 2012
Part 1

The aprons were so torn, thin and worn they weren't fit to use as rags, yet I couldn't bear to part with them. At least not at first. When one of the three finally ripped apart in the washing machine, however, I knew the time came. Gathering all, I reluctantly carried them to the large, white, cylinder-style garbage can. It had a rounded lid like an R2D2 Star Wars robot, and I stood in front of it for awhile, trying to build courage while cradling the material against my cheek.

I recalled a surprise snowfall one August while I stood by the barbeque grill on the ranch's porch. (College friend Katie was visiting that week. She was so astonished she had to call her family in Cleveland, Ohio on the radio phone.) I heard Rosie bellowing urgently as she paced the fence line, later delivering her calf right into my hands. There came a vision of groceries scattered all over the forest floor, the result of a sled's hitch popping off my snowmobile's ball. And I smiled wistfully at the comical image of my parents, riding in the wagon after being picked up at the trailhead. Dad was standing behind me (both hands on my shoulders), beaming with the sense of adventure, while Mom sat clutching the rough wooden sideboards with a death grip.

She never did like horses.

During their two-week visit, like a true engineer Dad drove everyone crazy. "Please get him out of our hair," one of the boys finally begged.

"He keeps telling us how to do things." We wracked our brains to come up with a project that would keep him occupied for a long, long time.

Nearly bursting from the sense of deception behind their request, the crew asked Dad to try and start the tractor, which had been sitting in the shed since who knew when. Completely covered with rust, spider webs, and burlap bags, it was so old the "tires" were metal. They reasoned, "We could use it! Maybe it can be hooked to the (equally-rusty) machinery that is scattered about the property. The meadow grass could then be mowed and dried for hay!"

Limping slightly from the after-effects of an ancient, Auburn University football injury, Dad set off across the yard. Except for meals —and a return trip to the trailhead to fetch his tool bag from the trunk—we didn't see much of him for nearly three days. But the pile of engine parts, laid out on an old sheet, continued to grow larger.

On the final evening he balked at coming to dinner. Knowing how completely focused he tended to get on projects, Mom encouraged crew and guests to start without him. "I've heard a whole lotta banging going on out there," one of them remarked with amusement.

Right about then came a whirring sound, kind of like a car makes when the engine won't turn over. Abruptly, everyone stopped talking and eating. The sound repeated several times and was followed by a roar. Silverware clanked when we rose and took off for the door as a unit.

Enveloped in a cloud of black smoke, Dad was in the metal driver's seat, ducking under the shed overhang, as the tractor backed out of the shed.

Twenty years of Idaho mountain memories were associated with those aprons. Giving them up was like saying good-bye to a lifestyle gone forever. I sighed and dabbed final tears with the thin, faded fabric, then quickly, like something might bite, stuffed them inside the can, cringing at the mixed whiff of coffee grounds, discarded food scraps and cat litter that wafted from the opening. Hurrying away, I covered my ears against the sound of the lid swinging back and forth, pushed open the screen door and fled to the yard.

Darby, my dog, came trotting up to lick me.

Other aprons followed the ones that were tossed. A black and white-striped one from a department store. Something checkered from a catalogue. A horse-patterned version from a Farmer's market. My newest Colorado friend, Peggy, also gifted a wonderful, pale green version with pink accents. "Seems like you always have one on," she pointed out when I sincerely thanked her. But although the quality was close, even that one wasn't as sturdy as Mom's. Material these days is much cheaper.

Come to think of it, everything's cheaper.

## Idaho
## Part 2

Dressed in slim-fit blue jeans, a flowered top, stylish summer jacket, and clogs, Adrianne stepped onto the porch of the lodge. "Hey, watcha' doin'?" she called in a raspy East Coast accent.

"Hanging laundry," I called back. Shortly after serving breakfast I'd begun the weekly process of sorting jeans, socks, shirts, sheets and towels. Several piles had been stacked outside of the shed which housed the washing machine. For nearly three hours I'd repeatedly hauled five-gallon buckets of water from my cabin's bathtub faucet and repeatedly heaved them into the generator-powered washer.

Heavy wicker baskets of wet garments had been lugged past the lodge to the clothesline. In-between lifting, shaking, and hanging them, I'd frequently paused to rub my lower back and admire the view. Snow still lingered on the highest peaks of the surrounding mountains. The meadow was as green as an emerald and bright with violets, Indian paintbrush and prickly pear. Three foals, and Rosie's calf, lay sprawled in the broodmare pasture taking mid-morning naps while their mothers grazed nearby.

Adrianne clomped down the wooden steps and across the yard. "Hangin' lawndry? For real?" she asked. Her frizzy chestnut hair had been pulled into a ponytail; it was untamable without access to a curling iron. Gazing upward, she added "Can I 'twy it?"

Over 30 feet long, that massive clothesline consisted of five strands of thick wire supported by three wooden T's made from railroad ties. It easily held six loads without sagging. "Sure." I dipped into my apron pocket and passed her a handful of clothespins.

She gave one a few, cautious test-snaps. "How does 'dis wuk?"

I demonstrated how to attach a towel to the line with one clip on either end and, "just in case the wind comes up this afternoon," a third in the center. Enthusiastically, Adrianne reached for a towel of her own. She didn't get the second clothespin attached very snugly, however, and it fell. When she stooped to part the grass and retrieve it, the towel came loose and dropped onto the back of her head. After a few more fumbles she backed up to admire her work, exclaiming. "Wow! 'Dis is wild!"

"Good job!" I said approvingly.

"Now whuh?" She looked around, noting the many garments hanging in neat rows.

I gestured to the basket. "There's plenty more..."

She bent and starting poking through the items, finally selecting a washcloth and clipping it with two pins. It was lopsided but acceptable. "Good! Good!" I exclaimed.

Around that time Adrianne's husband wandered by with his fly-fishing pole. "'Dere you ah! What cha'doin?" he asked.

"Harol'! Hey Harol'! Lookit, I'm hangin' lawndry!" She snatched for a second washcloth. Lifting both hands to the line she urged, "Hey, take my pi'chuh!"

Harold obligingly laid down his pole, lifted the camera that was strapped around his neck and snapped several shots while Adrianne posed. "You look great, baby," he remarked while advancing the film. Gesturing towards the jumbo-sized set-up, he asked incredulously, "You do 'dis all da time?"

"Yup." I had a few pins in my mouth by then and was wrestling with a sheet.

"Gheesh, lookit all dem socks! You gotta hang 'em *awl*?"

"Sure do. There are lots of guys on the ranch crew..."

"He-uh, lemme take some," Adrianne offered enthusiastically. She gathered a handful and carried them to the section which held several dozen others. The socks were nearly identical, some with blue stripes, some with black, and some red. "How do'ya tell dese apart?" She asked, frowning slightly as she began awkwardly clipping, one pin to each sock.

"I leave them on the line and let the boys decide what's what." I didn't tell her that sometimes, two or three mismatched strays remained dangling until the following wash cycle, unclaimed.

"Oh." She posed again, insisting over one shoulder, "Here! Harol'! Take anudduh! I never seen so many socks in my *life*!"

Harold took a few more shots before reattaching the lens cap. "'Das enough, honey. I gotta go. Mike says 'd fish are bitin'."

"Wai'! I'm comin' wit' cha!" Like a switch had been shut off, Adrian abruptly returned her remaining socks. "'Tanks, 'dat was fun!" she exclaimed on her way by. A few feet later she stopped, came back, and dropped several clothespins into my pocket. "Nice apron," she remarked, nodding approvingly. "I haven' seen no lady wearin' one of 'dose since my gran' mudduh died."

I smiled and fondly smoothed the apron, which reached from chest to knees. It *was* nice — and over the years had been useful for so many more things than just holding clothespins.

My mother made three, nearly identical versions and sent them after I took the ranch job. They were sewn out of medium-heavy denim, trimmed with red rickrack, with two, deep, double-stitched pockets in front. They arrived via mail plane, and since holidays were a long way off I was instantly curious after the pilot passed the box into my arms.

There was no note, but I knew immediately how much time and love had gone into those treasures. Unfolding the top one, I envisioned Mom sitting in our basement at her own mother's 1930's style, single-stitch machine. Although there was no desire (or patience) to learn to sew at that point, I'd spent hours watching doll clothes, school clothes, dresses, shirts and handkerchiefs taking form underneath the humming, rhythmic needle.

In the late 1960's, my sister and I were gifted with matching aprons (Mom made one for herself, too) embroidered with our names. Easy-Bake ovens were the rage for little girls around that time, so that's where the first practice-cooking experiences took place. I've been wearing aprons ever since.

Those that arrived in the backcountry were made with extra-long ties that could be wrapped around the back and tied in front, so they were figure-flattering as well as practical. Every morning when I slipped into the kitchen, the first thing I did was lift one from the hook beside the pantry and ease it over my head like a uniform. Those uniforms draped like liquid armor, forming a shield from the endless, assorted messes of full-scale ranch cooking from sourdough starter to bacon splatter to confectioner's sugar. They repelled blood when I gutted fish or butchered meat. They provided barriers against the soot, grease, and glue-like resins from Maggie.

An apron was useful for shooing any horses or mules that slipped into the yard. (A couple of them were adept at unlatching the main gate with their lips.) I whirled one over my head and snapped at their rumps until they trotted in the direction of the meadow. Same when the hens crept onto the back porch, trying to sneak cat food.

Holding the corners with one hand, I fed chickens by scooping their scratch into the pouch it formed and scattering it across the yard. While they were busy pecking I checked nests and gathered eggs, carefully placing each within the fold so none would crack as they were carried to the lodge. After the milking was finished, I wiped excess udder balm off my hands against the fabric.

In an apron I organized, boxed, packed and restocked supplies for three drop camps in addition to the lodge, cleaned saddles, filled lanterns with kerosene, swabbed the outhouse, or lugged wheelbarrows of wood from the shed. (Bonus, an apron prevented sawdust and woodchips from falling down the pants.) I also cut, sliced, chopped, pounded, measured, kneaded, fried, poured and stirred until my hands ached.

But one afternoon, an apron made by Mother saved my life.

Maggie had been snapping and popping since early afternoon while I started supper. Since *everything* was made from scratch, dirty mixing bowls, pans, muffin tins, and an assortment of non-electric utensils cluttered the counter. For convenience — it's surprising how much hot water is needed each day — I kept a jumbo-sized pot of water on Maggie to use for clean-ups. Now taking a firm grip on both handles, I heaved the pot up and with short, careful steps started walking towards the sink.

Abruptly, one of my cowboy boots slid on the linoleum. Hot water swirled within the pot as my arms jerked back and forth. Struggling to stay upright, I lurched, swayed and juggled for several long, breathless moments...then in slow motion lost all control.

Boiling liquid slammed directly into my chest and flinging the pot, I screamed at the top of my lungs. Cascading downward, steaming water spread across the floor with a *whooooosh*. All alone in the middle of nowhere, the only choice was to spring into emergency mode.

Whipping the apron over my head, clawing at the buttons of the flannel shirt beneath it, pulling and throwing both that and a tee off, hopping first on one foot then the other to drag off both boots, then peeling out of my blue jeans, I bolted for the bathroom, turned the faucet on full-blast, and stepped into the tub to run cold water on the burns.

Repeatedly cupping both hands and splashing the raw skin, I crouched there for at least a minute, terrified, mind racing. When was everybody going to be back? Was there enough burn cream in the first aid kit to use over such a large area of injured skin? Where *was* the first aid kit? Didn't the boys take it to their cabin in search of band-aids? Should I call the Cascade hanger, tell them there was an emergency, and arrange for a flight to a Boise hospital? But…slowly…it dawned on me: there was no pain. Was it true that it didn't sink in right away due to shock?

Puzzled, I stopped splashing myself and carefully scanned arms, torso and legs. There were no bubbling blisters. To be sure, I tentatively poked a finger here and there to check for stinging sensations. Nothing. Astonished, I straightened. Water continued to pour out of the faucet and gather around my feet. *What? I was okay?* Finally shutting it off, like a sleepwalker I stepped out onto the mat and wrapped up in a towel.

It was only after returning to the kitchen, barefoot, that I realized what had happened. A blue blob lay in the middle of the puddle that was slowly spreading under the bar stools, the wood box and the kitchen table. I retrieved the dripping apron and held it out, staring in disbelief upon realizing it had just saved me from serious harm by completely repelling the scalding liquid.

I gathered the rest of the also-soaked garments, slid into a pair of rubber boots, walked to my cabin, and put on dry clothes. Back at the lodge, the floor was scrubbed from one end to another — even furniture was moved. The hunters tracked their muddy boots across it later, but for once it didn't matter. And nothing was said to them about the close call and the apron. Somehow it was so personal, and so kin to being protected by an angel, I had to keep it to myself.

It wasn't the first time I'd felt humbled in the mountains.

All these years later, I'd probably still be on that ranch if the foreman hadn't been so bad at managing and book keeping. The end result was a change of ownership. Right away, the new people began to formulate drastic changes. They dabbled in notebooks, drew diagrams, and clumsily attempted all sorts of important calls on the radio phone. ('Clumsily' because on a system like that, people not only have to take turns talking but they must allow for three to five-second delays between responses.) I overheard something about tearing down my rustic cabin (as well as the outhouse and shed) because several new ones were to be built. Legal paperwork was drawn up for the ranch to become a dues-only/

members-only establishment. One dummy even came up with the idea of smoothing a huge section of meadow for a golf course.

"Guess they've never heard of ground squirrels," one of the guides mumbled, rolling his eyes. "At least there'll be plenty of holes."

The four Californians who'd bought (and eventually lost) it — a pool builder, a lawyer, a brick mason, and a restauranteur — never had a chance: they didn't know which end of a mule ate the hay, they just needed an investment. "I've always wanted a summer home in the wilderness," the pool builder told me confidently, during his second visit. "I was an Indian in a past life. I need to be standing on a mountain top with the wind blowing through my hair."

'Well, that wind is sure gonna push you plumb off!' I remember thinking to myself, looking down at him with a mix of disbelief and dismay.

One by one the guides quit. I remember saying good-bye to them all, knowing we'd never see each other again. But I was willing to stay and give things a try. Not too long afterwards, however, one of the Californians brought his brassy, spoiled city niece in to cook because she, too, wanted to live in the mountains. So did her lazy husband.

When their two, small boys got bored after exploring the place and started tossing rocks at the horses and chickens, I packed up and headed for town.

The tiny house was in the woods between Lake Fork and Donnelly, so far off the main road the city didn't plow. I had to gun my truck sideways in 4-wheel drive, spraying mud or snow, to get in or out. The sole neighbor was a surly, hermit-like Vietnam vet who plowed, when he felt like it, in exchange for filling his water jugs from my pump house. His trailer had no indoor toilet. His freckle-faced, ten-year-old daughter introduced herself by knocking on the sliding glass door and announcing, "Hi, I'm Spring. Can I come in?" before marching right past me.

I had two acres of pasture for three horses, endless dirt roads and forests to explore on them, a wood stove to heat and cook with, a job in a veterinary clinic, and a quiet country lifestyle with no streetlights or traffic sounds. In the fall one heard bull elk bugling. Some nights, the sky came alive with Northern Lights. It was as close to backcountry life as I could get (only without the guests) and I was happy.

Once again the aprons came in handy as I pulled weeds, planted flowers, tightened barbed wire, put polyurethane on hardwood floors, and painted both the inside and the outside of the house. When I started a dog-sitting business, aprons were the barriers between slobber, hairs, and muddy paw prints. When I began cleaning houses for extra money, they caught the dust I wiped off walls, cabinets, and bookshelves and the dried food scrubbed off stove and counter tops. And after I sold that first house and moved into a 300' rental trailer (while shopping for a second one), they protected me from the mouse droppings and dead bugs that had accumulated from it being empty for so long.

"I don't recall seeing you without an apron on...do you *ever* take them off?" one of seven dinner guests joked one evening. It happened at the first house, where everyone was happily crammed at a round, clawfoot table. Side dishes were being set on a trunk in the corner, mere inches away.

"Nope," I smiled, shifting things around to add a bowl of freshly-mashed potatoes. Glancing down, I noticed a blob had landed on the fabric, so I scooped it with a finger and put it in my mouth. "Doesn't *everybody* wear them?"

Colorado

Part 3

I had a steady job here with a weekly periodical called the Western Slope Fence Post, and through it started a column called "Living the Good Life." One afternoon, stopped cold by writer's block, I decided to tell the story of mother's aprons and the day one saved me. She subscribed to the magazine, so I knew she'd read it, but the issue came and went without her saying a single word. Instead, as usual, during our monthly long-distance calls she prattled on and on about the weather, the neighbors, her Bridge club, and her favorite movies.

But about a year after the original version of "Apron Strings" was published, another surprise box from Mother arrived in the mail. This one was heavy, delivered by a pony-tailed woman who drove a jeep with a flashing orange light on the hood.

Wearing a sleeveless gardening dress protected by one of the store-bought aprons, I curiously lugged that box into the house, set it on the counter, fetched a knife, and opened it. There was no note although I searched for one, carefully poking about the newspapers she'd used for packing.

Underneath those newspapers were two brand-new denim aprons — this time, trimmed in blue rick-rack. Stunned, I gasped and stepped backwards, one hand on my mouth, before gently lifting the top one out, unfolding it, holding it to my body and looking down.

Again, the memories flooded, this time taking me back to the day I'd left home for Idaho. The truck bed had been loaded with luggage, a cooler, water, extra oil, a jack, and my sleeping bag. Tee was pawing in the horse trailer; Dad took a picture of me standing by the open side window with her head peeking out. He also got a shot of me tearfully cuddling our family's beloved Siamese cat, Tony.

I hugged Dad after posing for those pictures, and we awkwardly stood in the driveway waiting for Mom. When she finally appeared in her housedress and Keds sneakers, her eyes were red and her own, home-made apron had damp spots. Yet both arms were extended and she was smiling bravely. "Ba'h ba'h, Hunneh," she said in an Alabama accent that was still strong after her own two decades in Ohio. She lightly patted my back, adding "You take ca'uh."

Climbing into the cab and reaching for the seatbelt, I took a deep breath to calm excitement and briefly wondered why on earth, considering the occasion, they didn't sob in my presence and say, "I love you, don't go" ...but it wasn't their way.

My parents raised my older brother, sister and me to be responsible. Pay our bills. Know the difference between needs and wants. Make do with what you have on hand. Wipe the dust of your britches and get on with it. And take a job that can support you...something steady, like teaching. After all, what else could one do with a mere English degree?

So...no...come to think of it, even if Mom and Dad had begged me not to leave for guide school, I'd still have pulled away. Unlike my brother, who is an anesthesiologist, and my sister, who teaches Special Needs children, I was the one who marched to a much different drummer.

They knew it and let me go, choosing instead to stand in the driveway, smile stoically, and wave before returning to their gardening and canning.

Dad died in 1988. Mom was already in her nineties when she made those last two aprons, yet every stitch was perfect. I marveled at the seamstress work, turning them over and over in my hands. She *had* read the Fence Post story. She *had* understood what the others meant to me. Lovingly, I placed both into a sideboard drawer. They are only worn on special occasions now, and I wash them by hand because they need to last. We lost Mom in December.

But there was something else tucked into that box. At the bottom was a large, brown grocery bag which was as faded, torn, and worn as the original aprons had been. Puzzled, I eased it out with both hands.

Inside was every, single letter I'd ever written home after leaving Ohio, some containing pictures. Opening the top one, I read from lined, white paper marked with pencil,

Dear Mom and Dad,

Tee and I have made it to Kamiah. She rode fine until the last 100 miles, then she started kicking the sides which made the truck rock. I guess after five days on the road she was tired of being cooped up in the trailer...

The grocery bag ripped slightly as I reached inside to scoop out more. There were a least a hundred. Filled with wonder I read six of them, marveling at the free-spirited and fearless girl I once was.

Am.

Right away, I knew just what to do with those letters.

*"Mother's home-made aprons were — and are — both attractive and functional."*

# BIOGRAPHY

Carolyn White is the pseudonym of Carolyn Coleman Waller. Born and raised in Marietta, Ohio, she is a graduate of Ohio University with degrees in English and Creative Writing. She has been freelancing as a feature reporter, photographer, and columnist since 1986 and currently contributes to *The Rocky Mountain Fence Post, IDAHO, Farm Show,* and *The Beacon.* Her work has also appeared in *Colorado Central, The Natural Horse, Montrose Style* and many other magazines. She lives in Colorado with her husband, John, two dogs and three cats. "Brick underneath a Hoop Skirt" is the first book in a series.

Additional copies of "Bricks underneath a Hoop Skirt" can be purchased for $15.50 each (includes postage and handling) at:

**Unleashed Publishing Co.**
**C. C. Waller**
**P.O. Box 612**
**Cedaredge, Colorado 81413**

CPSIA information can be obtained
at www.ICGtesting.com
Printed in the USA
LVOW10*0820200618

581353LV00013B/268/P